To A Rising
ST★R !

(signature)

Cover design by Karina Wijaya
Interior design and illustrations by Tiffany Leeson

Published by the Enterprise Development Group, Inc.

Learn more information at:
www.enterprisedevelop.com

Creating Value
with CO-STAR

An Innovation Tool
for Perfecting
and Pitching
Your Brilliant Idea

A Practical Guide
for Innovators

Laszlo Gyorffy
and
Lisa Friedman

Dedicated to innovators everywhere,

working to solve the world's important problems;

and to entrepreneurs and pioneers

with positive visions for the future.

Creating Value with CO-STAR

An Innovation Tool

for Perfecting

and Pitching

Your Brilliant Idea

Laszlo Gyorffy
and
Lisa Friedman

CONTENTS

Preface

Decoding the Magic of Innovation

There is a special kind of **magic** when it comes to innovation: Innovators working inside and outside companies create the next generation of products and services. Young entrepreneurs appear seemingly out of nowhere to start companies that transform the world. Seasoned "serial entrepreneurs" innovate over and over again. Their breakthrough ideas are often surprising and deliver hope for a better future: they find funding where others languish; they open new markets and sometimes give birth to entirely new industries. While it may appear that their success is all about creative new ideas, successful innovators know how to take raw ideas through a series of iterations, all the way to implementation and value creation.

At the Enterprise Development Group (EDG), we've had the great fortune to work with a number of these masters of innovation and to learn the secrets of their craft. For the past two decades we have consulted with a large number of clients to help them implement proven innovation practices throughout their organizations. Sometimes our clients even use these practices across the boundaries of their enterprise to innovate with customers and alliance partners. In some cases we have provided support to entire innovation "ecosystems" or regions that want to create a focused innovation economy.

We have learned from the best, both from innovators and from those who fund them, and we have gathered their secrets into a set of simple innovation best practices that anyone can learn. Game-changing innovation often looks like magic, but behind this success there is most often a very structured series of steps, a "discipline of innovation." Entrepreneurs, innovators, and funders can use a few simple steps to evolve ideas that have significant positive impact in the market—and on the bottom line.

CO-STAR:

An
Innovation
Tool
that
Enhances
Value

Customer

Opportunity

Solution

Team

Advantage

Result

CO-STAR is a tool for creating compelling
value propositions that lies at the heart
of this set of innovation best practices.

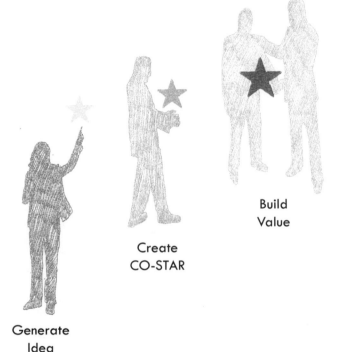

Realize
Dream

Build
Value

Create
CO-STAR

Generate
Idea

CO-STAR
condenses the most
essential steps in
creating customer
value into one
simple-to-use formula.

This CO-STAR guide is intended to provide you
with a practical set of practices for:

Identifying significant innovation opportunities.

★

Generating creative solutions.

★

Developing your value proposition.

★

Communicating your idea in a clear and compelling manner.

★

Creating cost-effective prototypes.

★

Collaborating effectively with colleagues to rapidly improve your idea.

I n the current fast-paced marketplace, there is good news and bad news. The **bad** news is that creating something out of nothing is difficult. Technologies, products, services, and business models are changing exponentially quickly. Global competition is more intense than you could even imagine. The odds are stacked against you.

The **good** news is that there has never been a better time to innovate. In today's hyper-connected world, access to helpful information and tools is unprecedented. Innovation is not restricted to the lone genius—innovation is a mindset and skill set we can all master. While some individuals may be naturally gifted, everyone has the capacity to discover problems that need to be solved, to think creatively, and to use tools to facilitate their innovation efforts to produce positive results. This book offers you a simple and straightforward set of practices to significantly **increase your chance of success.**

Note from the Authors

We have been asked to write this short guide by clients and colleagues for years. We recognize that one of our greatest contributions to assisting idea generators is in the front end of the innovation process. It is during the formative stage where a simple yet thorough thinking tool can have the most impact, at the lowest cost.

We hope that CO-STAR contributes to the launch of solutions that we all need, solutions that we will be happy, and proud, to have facilitated. As a society, we face many challenges in our economies, in our communities and countries, in our environment, and in how we live and work together across boundaries. We hope that CO-STAR helps innovators to integrate collective intelligence into their ideas, as a step in helping them create enduring value.

We would love to hear from you—let us know what you are "CO-STARring"!

Laszlo Gyorffy
and Lisa Friedman,
August 2012

Enterprise Development Group,
Palo Alto, California USA
+1 650 855-9940

www.enterprisedevelop.com

About the Authors

Laszlo Gyorffy, M.S. is President of the
Enterprise Development Group (EDG), an international consulting and training firm headquartered in Palo Alto, California, in the heart of Silicon Valley. For over twenty years, Laszlo has worked with organizations around the globe to "expand the possible." He has enabled clients to refocus, redesign, and re-energize their business strategies and innovation practices to succeed in an increasingly demanding marketplace. Laszlo also creates and delivers transformative training programs. In the Innovation Advantage training, business leaders learn to build an innovation culture and architecture to dramatically improve the odds of their company launching commercially successful products. Laszlo is also the lead architect for EDG's Q+ online innovation platform, which blends the best of social media with innovation best practices to tap the creative genius of an entire enterprise.

Lisa Friedman, Ph.D. is a co-founder of EDG and
co-author of *The Dynamic Enterprise: Tools for Turning Chaos into Strategy and Strategy into Action*. She works with business leaders globally to facilitate a shared understanding of the emerging trends transforming their industries, to shape vision and strategy for the future, to teach simple but powerful innovation practices, and to align their organizations and engage their people to reach the future they envision. She is a frequent speaker and workshop leader on re-imagining business for the digital era, innovation best practices, future-driven leadership, and eco-innovation. She is an editor for the *International Journal of Innovation Science*, based in the U.K. Lisa also leads EDG's client exchanges and customized innovation tours, bringing leaders from around the world to Silicon Valley to explore the game-changing innovations most relevant to their current strategy. Lisa Friedman and Laszlo Gyorffy are co-creators of EDG's Qandu Integrated Innovation System that enables companies and industry networks to innovate quickly and effectively. CO-STAR is one of the primary tools that makes the Qandu System so successful.

Are you a champion for change?

Who?
What?
Why?
When?

1

The Who, What, Why, and When of CO-STARring with Your Idea

Who Should CO-STAR?

CO-STAR is a simple, powerful formula for focusing on the ultimate value of an idea: a "value proposition." But it is not for everyone. Ask yourself:

* Are you an entrepreneur? Are you someone with an idea for a new business?

* Are you an intrapreneur? Are you someone working in an organization with an idea for how to create new customer value?

* Are you a champion for change? Do you see how a product, service, practice, or policy could be radically improved? Or how it could be redesigned or reinvented altogether?

* Are you willing to invest your own time, energy, and creativity in championing your idea to the point where it gets approved, funded, sold, licensed, implemented, adopted or launched into the world?

If you answered **"yes"** to any of these questions then this book will help you get started. Committing to your idea is the first step in what could be a remarkable journey for you, your customers, and possibly the world. This book is for dreamers and difference-makers. Welcome to the team.

Managing the Paradox of Innovation

As a committed champion of your idea, you will need to manage the duality and often paradoxical nature of the innovation process—you will need to bring discipline to a creative act. CO-STAR is a thinking-and-doing tool that allows you to blend and balance the multiple demands of invention.

While everyone's journey is different, we have found over the years that you will be required to manage a number of contradictions. You will be required to:

* Be passionate and committed yet willing to let go as it becomes necessary and appropriate.

* Build a vision of the future while working in the present.

* Gather broad input while staying focused on delivering specific results.

* Develop personal ideas while maintaining the perspective of the customer.

* Stay the course and stay committed while continuously seeking feedback and allowing evolution.

* Be knowledgeable and confident yet willing to admit to not knowing something.

* Be willing to take chances while working to reduce business and product risks.

* Be willing to think outside the box while working within the confines of an organization's or network's strategy and structures.

* Take personal ownership for your ideas while building a sense of shared responsibility within the team and ecosystem.

Innovation always starts with someone committing to an idea and demonstrating leadership from beginning to end. If these challenges sound motivating to you, you are ready to develop your value proposition.

What is **CO-STAR?**

CO-STAR is our unique formulation of a value proposition. The value proposition is a crisp and compelling description of how you intend to bring benefit to a specific customer group in a way that delivers far more value than competing alternatives. Some value propositions may be similar to existing products, services, or business models, but with new features that customers care about; while others may be bold game-changing offers that disrupt the marketplace.

By now quite a few useful templates are available for creating a good value proposition (see Barnes et al.'s *Value Proposition Builder,* Guy Kawasaki's ten questions [2004], or SRI's NABC— Need, Approach, Benefit, and Competition [Carlson and Wilmot, 2006]). We have studied and practiced many of these methods and have condensed the elements we consider most essential into CO-STAR.

CO-STAR focuses on the key elements that turn an idea into a value proposition:

C—Who are the intended Customers and what is their important unmet need?

O—What is the full potential of the Opportunity?

S— What is your proposed Solution for capturing the Opportunity?

T— Who needs to be on the Team to ensure the Solution's success?

A— What is your Solution's competitive Advantage over the alternatives?

R— What Results will be achieved from your Solution?

CO-STAR provides a framework for crystallizing your thinking and a vehicle for collaborating with others to enhance the value of your idea. It:

* Provides an easy-to-use discipline for idea development and value creation.
* Allows for quick and focused evaluation and exchange of helpful opinions.
* Establishes the critical components of a business plan from the very beginning.
* Shapes a winning pitch for funders or sources of approval and resources.

Fundamentals of Value Creation

Who defines the value of your idea? Others may have an opinion, but at the end of the day, the customer defines value.

The power of the CO-STAR template comes from its a priori establishment of a customer-driven business case. The basic rule is this:

no customer = no value = no innovation
It's as simple as that.

Why CO-STAR?

Whether you are employed in a large company or a small business, performing science in a lab, serving your country in the government, working in a nonprofit, or looking to start your own business or organization, every innovator must understand two truths:

1. The idea you generate must deliver value. Being able to crystallize your thinking and determine the true value of your idea is critical to success. Without understanding the fundamentals of value creation you may find you are pushing an idea no one wants. Before an idea can become great, its brilliance must be understood. What value does it deliver that makes it extraordinarily attractive to customers and its potential market?

2. At some point you will need help with your idea. No one does any kind of significant innovation on his or her own. No one has all of the necessary skills and resources. While inventors may enjoy brilliant sparks of insight, innovation is inherently a social activity. Thus, you must be able to effectively communicate your idea and collaborate with others to improve your thinking, gather support, secure funding, and put your idea into action. More often than not, ideas start in an unfinished state. Many good ideas even start out as "bad" ideas. Yet, every seemingly bad idea, when tested and iterated by a community of committed collaborators, may well become the Next Big Thing.

We believe you make your own luck. Identify and pursue enough good opportunities and you will be rewarded. The rewards are both intrinsic and extrinsic and vary in importance from person to person. Rewards can include new skills, new relationships, more meaningful work, learning about topics that interest you, creative expression, advancing your career, recognition for achievement, personal growth, unprecedented teamwork, a sense of accomplishment and fulfillment, a feeling of being part of something important, and sometimes even wealth.

> ## "I saw the angel in the marble and carved until I set him free."

Michelangelo (1475–1564)
(BrainyQuote.com, 2011)

Michelangelo was able to look beyond the rough edges of an early creation and see its value. Imagine if you and your colleagues could do this as well.

When Should You CO-STAR?

From the Very Beginning

In the beginning, all ideas of any significance are incomplete, inexact, and inadequate. The seeds of brilliance may be present, but a rigorous nurturing process is needed before your idea can flower in full beauty. Iteration is key. Idea development depends on continual discovery—on collecting, sifting, discarding, building. Every idea starts as a fragment that needs to evolve. By beginning to CO-STAR right from the start, you can make the collecting, sifting, and developing process much more straightforward, much more organized, and that much easier. As you continually process your ideas through the filter of CO-STAR, your consciousness will naturally focus ever more keenly on the aspects of your idea that are really important, the aspects that deepen the value of your idea and ultimately take you to where the gold of your idea resides.

It's a particularly good practice to write down your initial CO-STAR ideas wherever you can, whether it's on the back of a napkin or in the notes section of your smartphone. The act of writing will bring greater clarity to your thinking, help you remember the concept, and begin preparing you to share your thinking with others. Don't worry that your CO-STAR is incomplete—everyone's first pass is incomplete.

Different CO-STARs for Different Audiences

You may need more than one CO-STAR, as you will often need to create different versions for different audiences. For example, a potential customer would need to see a different value proposition than a potential investor would see.

CO-STARs for Big Ideas

Big ideas are harder to conceive and easier to kill, because they are typically more risky. The greater the risk, the higher the hurdle. Proposing big ideas requires a very disciplined value creation process. Using a tool like CO-STAR to guide your thinking and communication can increase your chances for success, as you build your case that your big idea is worth the risk.

Think about how much innovation Henry Ford had to do to pursue his big dream:

1. Core technology: invented the combustion engine.

2. Product: invented the Model T.

3. Manufacturing process: invented the assembly line to build the Model T.

4. Business model: invented the national dealerships to incentivize sales and distribute cars.

CO-STARs for Industries in the Midst of Revolution

CO-STAR can be particularly helpful at times of disruption in an industry, when a great deal of innovation is needed all at once. For example, many industries are in the midst of major transformation, as they redefine themselves in the digital era or for the Green revolution. They are questioning their own industries: What is a newspaper? What is a book? How do we make or buy music? What kind of health tracking devices can we use at home? What kinds of energy will we use in the future? What are Green materials?

Innovators can use CO-STAR to help them create solutions for industries in the midst of transformation.

When many individual innovators share the same tools and language for value propositions, they can collaborate with each other more easily.

It is easier to get feedback, to form teams quickly, and to collaborate and find partners for innovations.

Leaders in companies and organizations face innovation challenges as well. Their innovators may be proposing 101 ways to imagine a book in the digital era, or to evaluate and track what makes materials Green, but only some of these ideas can be funded and moved forward.

So how can companies and organizations ensure they are selecting the strongest innovations? By using CO-STAR—it is a tool for innovators as well as leaders in organizations who want to invent the future.

Getting Started

2.

Getting Started: How to Turn Initial Ideas into Value Propositions

A typical CO-STAR effort begins as follows:

Step 1.

Write down your initial thoughts in the CO-STAR format. (See CO-STAR template on page 134). Reflect on what you discover about your idea and decide if it is worth pursuing. If so, proceed to Step 2.

For example, say you are an innovator and have one of those "light-bulb moments." You come up with a product idea that will dramatically cut lighting costs while also being better for the planet. You know a little about the industry and are willing to make some assumptions and estimates. An early draft of your "Seeing the Light" CO-STAR might look like this:

Customer
* Consumers and businesses who want to reduce their electric bill through more sustainable illumination.

Opportunity
* Lighting is a $100 billion industry worldwide, where sales of traditional incandescent light bulbs have steadily declined over the last five years.
* Semiconductor costs are going down so the Seeing the Light bulb will get cheaper at a time when the world is looking for more efficient and sustainable energy solutions.
* Governments around the world have passed measures to phase out incandescent light bulbs for general lighting in order to promote more energy-efficient lighting. Customers have to find new lighting solutions.

Solution

* The Seeing the Light bulb is a special, high-performance light bulb based on light-emitting diode (LED) technology, where the semiconductor made of one negatively charged layer is bonded to a positively charged layer. When electricity is introduced, electrons leave the negative layer for the positive layer to combine with atoms that have a missing electron. Light is emitted through the combination.

* We have found a unique way to manufacture this bulb at half the cost of other LEDs. Customers prefer LED light bulbs because they last longer and save energy, but they often are reluctant to buy them because the bulbs are so expensive. Our special manufacturing process cuts the price of LEDs substantially, making them much more attractive to customers.

Team

* We have a senior team with years of experience in the lighting industry. I will provide project management and product design expertise; Anna P. will lead the LED product development team; Jessie D. will lead the manufacturing team; and Terry K. will lead distribution and sales.

Advantage

* Over incandescent bulbs: The Seeing the Light bulb is more durable than standard incandescent bulbs, which have fragile filaments, and it lasts 100 times longer. Also, the sale of 110 watt incandescent bulbs will be banned by January 2012, and all incandescent bulbs over 40 watts will be banned by 2014.
* Over compact fluorescent lights (CFLs): The Seeing the Light bulb contains no toxic mercury, is dimmable, and lasts many times longer than CFLs.
* Over other LEDs: The Seeing the Light bulb is 50% cheaper than other LED bulbs for the same performance.

Results
* Without making any changes to a business customer's infrastructure, the long lifespan of the Seeing the Light bulb reduces labor costs due to fewer purchases and installations.
* A family could install Seeing the Light bulbs in their newborn's bedroom and not need to replace the bulb until that child went to college. The family also would have prevented 870 tons of carbon dioxide going into the atmosphere, as the bulbs use much less electricity to produce light.

Once you get feedback on your initial CO-STAR, you can begin to amend it to make it stronger. If you decide your value proposition has potential, proceed to Step 2.

Step 2.

Share your initial thoughts with a few trusted colleagues. Listen and learn from their reactions and feedback. Encourage them to tell you what they like about your idea and what could make it stronger. Ask them to comment separately on each part of your CO-STAR. What do they think about your Customer, Opportunity, Solution, Team, Advantage, and Results? This feedback is "gold"— learn as much from it as you can. Once you've considered the comments carefully, if there is still some juice to the idea, proceed to Step 3.

Step 3.

This pass requires research and quantification. Integrate the feedback you have already received and begin to answer the CO-STAR questions more thoroughly. Then take your idea out to a more objective audience to test its viability and potential. Repeat Step 2, following a pattern of iteration of 2—3, 2—3, 2—3, until the value proposition either evolves to where it can be implemented, or can be discarded because its value just can't be proven through the various tests.

You can work CO-STAR from two directions:

1. Start with market opportunity and develop a viable solution.
2. Have an energizing insight and then determine if this might be relevant for an actual customer need, or whether there is a viable market for your idea.

Guiding Principles

Active Exploration
The Internet is a remarkable vehicle for exploring and understanding the world. Use it. Use your online social network as well. But don't forget to get out of your office and look around: observe, interact, prototype, test, collect.

Continuous Iteration
The goal of the iteration process is to maximize potential and minimize business risk for your idea. The first draft you present should always be a CO-STAR, and seek as much input into each CO-STAR element as you can get.

Relentless Quantification
We need to know: how many customers, how much better, how much faster, and how much cheaper. Quantification is critical to judging the potential value of your idea, calculating return, reducing risk, and limiting subjectivity. Just look at the impact the right numbers had in this Zappos.com example:

In 1999, Nick Swinmurn approached Hsieh and Lin with the idea of selling shoes online. Hsieh was initially skeptical, and almost deleted Swinmurn's initial voicemail. After Swinmurn mentioned that "footwear in the US is a $40 billion market and 5% of that was already being sold by paper mail-order catalogs," Hsieh and Lin decided to invest through Venture Frogs. Two months later, Hsieh joined Zappos as the CEO and has since doubled revenues every year, starting with $1.6 million in 2000. By 2009, revenues reached $1 billion. (Wikipedia.org, 2011)

Change the Game
The bar is high for disruptive innovation. This means your CO-STAR must be even stronger if you intend to champion an idea with the potential to reinvent a company, category, or even an industry.

Celebrate Success
Acknowledge progress and have some fun. Besides recharging your battery, a light heart is often the doorway to creativity.

Who is the customer?

3.

The Elements of CO-STAR

Who is the Customer?

Customers comprise the heart and soul of any value proposition. Without committed customers, your idea will not go far. An innovator must make a conscious choice about which customer segments to serve and which to ignore. Your choice may change as you develop your CO-STAR, but it helps to put a stake in the ground. Once you have made a decision, your value proposition can be carefully crafted around a deep understanding of specific customer needs.

Your CO-STAR begins by answering the fundamental question, "Who are our potential customers?" The answer can be businesses, consumers, users, individuals and families, or citizens. How many potential customers are there? What are their relevant interests, motivations, and needs? What will they experience as valuable enough to buy and use? Your thorough and detailed understanding of customers is essential to develop an idea that is relevant to them and offers value greater than existing alternatives.

Try to describe the customer in detail; bring the customer to life. Go beyond typical demographics and capture the nuances in their profile. For example, "engineers" might be your target customer, but "software engineers who face time-to-market pressure because of rapidly shrinking product life cycles" gives much more information to help drive innovation.

The best ideas solve a fundamental need—not simply a want, but a need. A want is something customers think would be nice to have, but wouldn't go out of their way to buy. People must truly need what you plan to offer.

Fundamental questions for clarifying the nature and needs of your customers are:

* Who are your customers? What unique features define them?
* What are your customers' interests? What matters to them?
* What specific unmet need will your solution address? Or put another way, what is the problem you are trying to solve?
* How important is the need to your customers? Will addressing their need in a new way make a significant difference to them?

Tips for Clarifying the "C" of Your CO-STAR

Write down your customer's unmet needs in terms of problems to be solved. Rather than saying what the customer needs, which is often a repeat of the solution you intend to offer, describe the current issues the customer faces. For example: The customer lacks X, is frustrated by Y, or X is so slow it creates Z.

For example, if a food company is working on developing a brand and a distribution system for fresh locally grown vegetables, it would be tempting to list the customer need as: "Customers need fresh locally grown vegetables."

However, if the team behind this new offering really looks at customer needs, they may find new information that can impact the solution they have in mind. For example, they discover that many of their customers didn't grow up eating some of the vegetables that grow well in their local region, and thus don't know how to cook these vegetables. However, they also learn that their customers are curious and would like to learn how to prepare these foods. The team's early customer research finds that unfamiliar vegetables packaged with colorful, easy-to-prepare recipes helps motivate customers to buy a wider range of locally grown foods.

 ## Tips for Identifying Multiple Customer Groups

Sometimes you will have several types of customers, and it may be helpful to specify the needs for each customer group. You may need different CO-STARs when presenting to different groups, or you may need to clarify the different needs within one overall CO-STAR, depending on the presentation.

For example, a company selling large, expensive diagnostic medical equipment has three different customer groups who each have differing needs. Medical patients—the ultimate end-users of the equipment—are concerned with the comfort and length of the testing procedure. The doctors, nurses, and lab techs that operate the equipment are concerned with ease of use, along with reliability and accuracy of test results. Finally, the hospital administrators, who would actually purchase the equipment, are most concerned with price. The CO-STAR for the next generation of equipment from this company thus has to prove that its new solution can meet the needs of each customer group far better than its competitors can.

 ## Tips for Gathering Customer Insight

There are many ways to gather the customer knowledge that fuels innovation. In fact, the means of focusing on customers and their experience is itself undergoing rapid innovation. Below are some methods of connecting with customers in order to understand their needs.

Interviews, questionnaires, surveys, and polls

* Focus groups where a facilitator asks open-ended questions about customer or stakeholder experience of your service or product.
* "Unfocus" groups composed of diverse people offering differing perspectives.
* Storytelling: Ask users to tell you personal stories of their experience.
* Extreme user interviews with those who know the most and the least about your service or product.
* Structured questionnaires for quantitative data
* Quick polls on websites or via email.

Direct observation

Observation is helpful because your customers may not know what they need or may have trouble articulating it, particularly when you are interested in an area that may be new or unfamiliar to them.

* Watch a number of your customers interacting with your products and services, or with the activities you are interested in innovating. Observe customers in the natural environment in which they would use the products or services or where their activities occur.
* Shadow: Follow a single customer from beginning to end of their use of the product, or throughout an activity, and make in-depth observations.
* Shadow with verbal description: Ask your customer to describe their experience, moment to moment, as they engage in the activity you are observing.
* Observe extreme users: Observe your fans and fanatics, the people who love your products and services, customers who use them more than anyone else, or customers who use them in different ways.

* Capture: Take photos or videos of the customer during their experience.

Customers as observers

Give customers the camera, along with instructions for them to document the most important elements in their day, and how the product or service or activity in question impacts them.

Simulation

Try it out yourself—be the customer and try the service or product for a period of time. But remember, you are not necessarily the market. Just because you like peanut butter on your tacos doesn't mean the whole world does!

Co-create with customers

Jointly identify and solve problems together.

Keep asking: Why? Why? Why?

Soon you will come to the core challenge. With this insight you may come up with a single solution that can solve many problems at once. For example, a television media company noticed that viewership for several of its shows aimed at a young male audience was in steep decline. The first solution they considered was to innovate better shows for these young males. However, they stopped to understand their customers and ask why, before jumping in to innovate their solution:

* "Why?" Their first "Why?" showed that young males in this age group were spending fewer hours watching television overall. Creating more compelling shows would thus not solve their problem, because their audience members were not in front of their TV sets to notice.

★ "Why?" Their young male audience was spending more time with video games, watching media on the web, and creating their own content than they were spending on their sofas watching TV.

★ "Why?" The media company went further and asked "Why?" one more time. They began to recognize the growing need for activity and interaction in this audience. They did not just need to innovate the content of their shows to make better shows for young male audiences, but they needed to innovate the very concept of a show. How could they introduce gaming elements? How could they let viewers interact and participate over the web or on smartphones or tablets? How could users help direct the flow of the show?

These insights led the media company to search for innovation in a whole new area—multi-platform interactive media.

What is the opportunity?

What is the Opportunity?

In this section of your CO-STAR you are looking to determine the market potential of your idea. You have clarified the customer need, and now you want to assess the size and promise of the opportunity and clearly describe the market dynamics surrounding it. Investigate the customer, market, technology, and trends that support your thinking. It is here that you expand the possible and consider how you might capture a bolder and more inspired vision of what could be done. You should not settle for simply solving the immediate customer issue.

Typically, venture capitalists (VCs) look at how well you understand market conditions, then at the management team, and finally at the idea you are pitching. If you don't have a management team, they will help you build one, but if you don't understand the market deeply they won't even listen to your solution.

Market Dynamics

Value propositions are crafted for, and their solutions are implemented in, specific market environments. With a good understanding of the context for your solution you can conceive a stronger, more compelling CO-STAR. Clearly describe the market dynamics surrounding the opportunity, and show that you really understand the full context of your target market segment. Reveal the economic forces, industry disruptions, and technical and consumer trends your solution will leverage. Consider the following:

* What is the state of the current market and where is it heading?
* What is the size of the overall market as well as your target market?
* What are the significant technological and social trends, and how does your idea play into them?

* Who are the significant players in your target market and how might they support or compete with your solution?
* What is the competitive landscape and how does it impact on your solution?

Continuous scanning of the market is more important than ever due to the speed and complexity of our global, mobile, digital economy. New ideas and partners may emerge and provide the breakthrough you need to take your idea to a new level of performance and promise.

*   *   *   *

Shiny Versus Significant

Having an in-depth understanding of market opportunities will provide you with an early "Go/No-go" decision point. If you discover that the opportunity is not significant, you may decide not to proceed, or you may choose to go in a different direction. First, ask yourself if your shiny, new, super-cool solution is really important to anyone other than you. If you have determined a customer would really care, then the conversation shifts to scale. How many customers care? In general, the more customers, the bigger the market potential. And finally, consider timing. Is there sufficient pull from the market for a solution like yours? If there is pull, mobilizing support for your solution becomes much easier. In the equation form, it looks like this:

Market Size x Importance x Urgency = Significant Opportunity

During the first round, you will often have to rely on your gut instinct. Committing to a disciplined approach for looking at the real opportunity will save you from potential pain later on. On the other hand, the analysis of the opportunity may suggest that you are entering a previously unknown "white space." Looking at opportunity from the perspective of forecast and projection can help you and potential collaborators or funders to gain significant confidence, particularly if your idea is radical. After the second, third, or forth iteration of your CO-STAR, you should have quantifiable proof that your idea is in service of significant opportunity.

Reframe Your Opportunity

If you are not convinced that the opportunity is significant, try reframing your solution in a grander and more all-encompassing light:
* Could your solution be a platform or gateway to many other solutions?
* Could it set a new industry standard?
* Could you make adjustments to the solution so it is appealing to a different or much larger market segment?
* Could you reduce the features in the solution and offer it at a significantly lower cost?
* Could you address a more focused problem or a much larger customer issue?
* Could you take it to a global audience?
* Could you partner with someone else's solution to extend your reach and impact?
* Could you take your solution directly to the customer?
* Could you partner with a competitor?

Overall, the key question is:

How could you capture a bolder and more inspired vision of what could be done given the market opportunities you see?

★ Tips

* We recommend researching enough to categorize the target market into three buckets: mini-markets, medium markets, and mega-markets. Ignore the mini-markets. Medium markets can be interesting if you think you can play a major role in them. Overall, look for the mega-markets!

* Iterate back and forth between the "C" and "O" of your CO-STAR—they belong together. As you learn about your market, you may change the way you see your customer, and vice versa. For example, the customers for locally grown vegetables in the last section (see page 36) may be part of an emerging trend of "locavores"—individuals and restaurants that are developing an interest in locally grown food. They get to know their "bio-region." They talk with local farmers, who are their heroes. Potential customers may not just want a product (fresh vegetables), but they may want an experience, or even an identity. They may want to join a growing movement, to connect with others, to feel part of something exciting. How would understanding this larger market trend affect what customers might need? How would this open up new "Opportunities for Solutions"?

What is your solution?

What is Your Solution?

Finally, you get to talk about your idea by describing your proposed solution. This is the point where you articulate the specific idea you have for satisfying the identified need and seizing the opportunity. In this section of your CO-STAR, you clarify whether you are offering: a new product or service; an improvement of an existing product or service that makes an important contribution; a dramatically improved customer experience; a process that significantly streamlines or cuts costs and/or increases performance; a new business model that reshapes the market; or a combination of all of these.

At this point, after you have framed a compelling "CO," an important customer need paired with a significant market opportunity, you may already be clear on your first version of your proposed solution. If so, your goal will be to begin to frame this into your CO-STAR so you can communicate it to others, begin to gather feedback, and build collective intelligence into your solution. Your ultimate solution may actually look very different from your first idea.

Your goal in this section is to provide enough detail so you are confident in your own thinking and can engender confidence in others. You want the key aspects of your solution to be clear enough to allow others to see the potential value of your idea.

Can You Begin Your CO-STAR with the Solution?

Realistically, innovators often start with a potential solution and work backwards. They may intuitively understand a customer need or important market opportunity, but sometimes innovators are caught up by a new technology that has just become available and they see the chance to create something that has never existed before. They are in love with a new idea. They have a solution in search of a problem to solve.

If you begin with an idea—with a solution—it is important to go back to the beginning to validate your idea. Is there really an important customer need where your idea is the solution? Is there a worthwhile market opportunity? Answering these questions will slow you down from just charging ahead with your new idea, but this homework can help you "go slow to go fast." Understanding the most compelling "CO," can help you see opportunities for your idea that you may not have imagined before. This will help you transform your great idea into a full value proposition.

Clarifying Your Solution

For communication purposes, the description of your idea should be simple, relevant, and intuitively understandable. Use common terms to state concretely:

* What is the solution you are proposing?
* What are its key functions and features, inputs and outputs?
* Which business will you be in? What will be your business model?
* Which new technologies or intellectual properties (IP) are incorporated into your solution?
* Does your solution complement or displace an existing offering?
* Which parts of the customer's total unmet need does your solution solve or not solve?
* What kinds of assets or resources are required for your solution?
* What is the expected price range of your solution for the customer?
* What is the estimated total cost of your solution?

Very often, as you complete the "S" section in your CO-STAR, you will uncover areas that need further exploration. Don't spend too much time documenting every aspect early on in your development efforts. The goal is a "once over, lightly." Remember that your idea will evolve over time so there is no need to fall in love with your initial concept. You need to retain your ability to let go of parts of your idea as new and better possibilities emerge from your research and collaborations.

Brainstorming and Idea Generation to Develop Your Solution

Sometimes, once you have developed the "CO" of your CO-STAR value proposition, you will still be wondering what your solution might be. Many innovators and entrepreneurs begin with a problem to solve or identify a market opportunity that is calling out for solutions. They may not be clear at all about what possible solutions exist. If this is true for you, you may choose to brainstorm and look for potential solutions on your own, with a partner, with a small team or a large group, with your online community, or with a sequence of these.

Here are some idea-generation guidelines we have found helpful:

* Take each element of the customer need and market opportunity and generate a list of solutions that come to mind for
  each of these elements. Then put this list away, and start
  again. You will remember the most compelling potential solutions, and you will likely synthesize many of the best ideas
  into integrated solutions.

Ground rules for brainstorming:

- Everyone participates
- Stay focused on topic
- One person speaks at a time
- Record the ideas where everyone can see
- Go for quantity
- Listen and build on the ideas of others
- Wild ideas are OK
- Defer judgment
- Be quick and to the point
- Push yourself to generate a few wild ideas—concepts you would never dream of implementing. Until you record a few of these, you know you or someone else in the group is holding back and self-editing. Get out of the box and push for divergence, creativity, and fun.

Tips for Brainstorming Business Models

Sometimes your solution will be an improved product or service, or a new business, but many innovations will be business models that redefine existing businesses into completely new forms. Think of Zappos beginning to sell shoes over the web in 1999. Shoes weren't new, and selling shoes wasn't new, but the idea that shoes could be sold to people who had never tried them on was new. Three key levers to their business success were: 1) offering free shipping for both the purchase and potential return; 2) offering speedy delivery by keeping the shoes physically present in a warehouse and using expedited shipping services; and 3) offering a one-year window of time for returns. These three extra features gave customers the courage to order a pair of shoes they had never held in their hands or tried on their feet. In fact, these features gave customers the courage to try many pairs of shoes at once, many more than they might have carried home from a store. Given that many customers then kept these shoes, Zappos quickly grew from an online shoe store to being a full-service online retailer offering a wide range of clothing and household items. In 2009, Amazon bought Zappos for $1.2 billion.

Identifying a winning business model may lead you to rethink your solution and how it is positioned. Once you have clarified your "CO," you may want to brainstorm potential business models that could revolutionize the market for your idea. Here are a few to consider:

* Razor and blades model: The razor is inexpensive, but the blades cost a lot (e.g., Gillette). This model is also called the printer and cartridges model—sell the printer cheap, or even give it away with the purchase of a computer, and then charge a lot for ink cartridges (e.g., Hewlett Packard, Epson, Brother).

* Auction model (e.g., eBay).
* Subscription model (e.g., health clubs, Spotify).
* Direct-to-consumer model: cut out the middleman (e.g.,
  Amazon, Zappos, Travelocity, 23andMe genetic testing).
* Free, subsidized by advertising (e.g., Google).
* Free, subsidized by donations (e.g., Wikipedia).
* "Freemium": Free for a basic level, then charge fees for the
  full-service premium level (e.g., The New York Times online
  subscription).

We discovered another wonderful method for brainstorming business models from Franz Johansson's *The Medici Effect* (2006). Once you know the general direction of your potential solution, you can open up your thinking about it before settling in and deciding which business model works best. Write a list of your most basic assumptions about your solution. For example, if you were going to create a restaurant chain, you might say that your basic assumptions about a restaurant are that it has a menu, that a chef cooks, that it serves food, and that it charges money for its meals. Now take each assumption and reverse it:

* What would a restaurant with no menu look like?
  The chef could cook whatever he wanted for the evening—
  as a surprise meal for the customer—a bit like going to a
  friend's house for dinner.
* What would a restaurant with no chef look like?
  Customers could cook from the restaurant's recipes, using all
  of the restaurant's specialty equipment.
* What would a restaurant with no food look like?
  People could bring their own food and the chef would help
  them cook it.
* What would a restaurant look like that didn't charge
  money? Businesses could sponsor the meals for an evening in
  exchange for interacting with customers, or customers would

pay, but they each would choose how much to pay—assuming they wanted the restaurant to stay in business.

Hopefully you can see the pattern here. List all the assumptions of your solution, and then reverse them. This exercise will help you to innovate ways in which you could meet your customers' most important needs.

★ Additional Tips for Generating Your Solution

* Be honest with yourself in developing your CO-STAR. This will help you avoid getting caught with "tech push." Just because you can do something doesn't mean that you should do it. Your idea must create value for a customer.
* Think about what your customers really hope to achieve for themselves. Think about the outcomes they want from your solution. These are the elements you want to optimize to enhance the value of your solution.
* Don't try to make a less-than-perfect solution work. Try again with a new idea.

Who needs to be on the team?

Who Needs to Be on the Team?

Innovation is a team sport. No one can do it alone. Today's innovations typically require a collection of intelligence, experience, and expertise.

Besides intelligence about the idea itself, a team of experts is often essential to ensure your solution becomes a winner. Consider the ecosystem in which you operate and look for partners, suppliers, influencers, funders, and supporters beyond the walls of your own organization. Depending on your idea and approach, you may chose to form a loose network of part-time contributors, while other projects demand the formation of a fully committed, multidisciplinary "dream team."

For the purposes of developing your CO-STAR, identify the collaborators needed throughout the project, with particular emphasis on the start-up phase. Then attach the names of actual people you or others will contact and recruit. Consider:

* Who needs to be on your team to ensure your solution's success?
* What skills will you need? What technical, market, or business model skills will be required?
* What does each of your current team members bring to the table?
* What are their roles?
* What other relationships do you need? Consider the ecosystem or value network of your solution. What partners, suppliers, distributors, or communicators will your solution require to be successful?
* Who do you need on board to be credible with people that will support you?
* How will you attract great talent?

If you don't have an idea yet, consider hanging out with a new crowd. You may need a new team to help you find your solution.

If you want to come up with something truly game-changing, watch for the signals and listen with new ears for what is possible.

These may be your new teammates:

- Non-customers

- Fringe suppliers

- Rogue employees

- Inspired artists

- Zealous regulators

- Eccentric entrepreneurs

- Pioneering technologists

- Off-the-radar competitors

- Visionaries from other industries

- Counterparts from other countries and cultures.

Tips for Building and Nurturing Your Team

You should try to build teams with diversity—teams that know how to make the most of their range of skills, talents, and perspectives. For example, IDEO, the well-known design firm, advocates building teams of "T-Shaped" people—people with deep expertise in one area (the vertical line in the T), but who also collaborate well with others (the horizontal line in the T).

Have a mix of skills on your team, including:
* People who see the big picture as well as people who love the details.
* People who are aligned with the external marketplace as well as people who understand the internal workings of the organization.
* People who pay attention to the finances, people who pay attention to the technology and product quality, and people who connect with customers.

In other words, you want to cover all the bases in your team, to have a great mix of technical skills, business skills, and people skills.

"Point of view is worth an extra 80 IQ points." Alan Kay, pioneering computer scientist

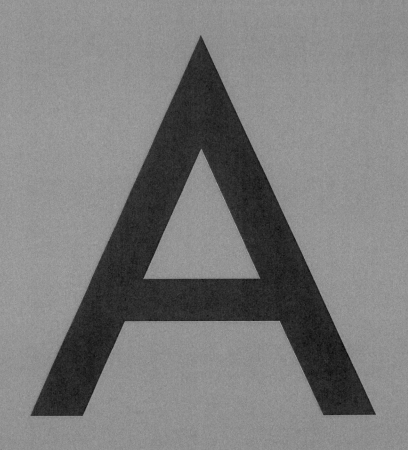

What is your advantage?

What is Your Advantage?

In this section you will perform a competitive analysis and define your "secret sauce"—the aspects of your idea that create a powerful competitive advantage over other alternatives. Remember, no matter how original your idea, there are always alternatives. The most obvious is to maintain the status quo and not buy or use your solution.

Defining the competition in non-traditional terms may help you define a distinctive position or rethink your solution. For example, Southwest Airlines defined its competition as the automobile, not other airlines. Southwest wanted to make flying so cheap and so simple, pleasant, and fun, that people would choose to fly rather than drive.

The goal is to identify the alternatives (e.g., glue versus anything that sticks things together) and the competitors (e.g., Coke versus Pepsi for soft drinks) and clarify the advantages your solution possesses.

Remember the old story about how NASA was going to design a pen that would write in space? The Russians defined the problem differently: How can we communicate on paper in space? They used pencils.

You are looking to determine how competitive your market space is and what your advantage is over the direct and even indirect competition. If your idea is a winner, others will try and copy it and eventually commoditize the offering. You will then be competing on brand and price. The bigger the lead you have, the longer the time to enjoy your first mover advantage. And bear in mind—it is a global marketplace and the bar is constantly being raised.

To assess your competitive advantage:

Generate a detailed list of specific alternatives and/or competitors, listing them by name.

* For each competitor and alternative, list all the ways in which your idea is superior.
* What are the most important advantages from a customer or buyer's perspective?
* The more specific and quantitative you can be, the easier the comparison. How much better, faster, or cheaper is your solution than the alternative?
* What is your protected IP that ensures your advantage over your competition?
* What makes your solution special? What is your "unfair competitive advantage" or your "secret sauce" that will make your customers love you?
* List all the ways your competitors or alternatives are superior. If they are superior in an area important to your customers, it is time to go back to the drawing board for your solution.
* What can you do to strengthen your solution over competing alternatives?

Be honest with your analysis and don't over-inflate the advantages of your solution. Understand the trade-offs and document the places where your solution may actually be inferior to a competitor. This can give you very important insight into ways to rethink your solution.

Finally, consider what is it about your idea that makes it pioneering. Describe the "secret sauce" that only you know how to mix. This gets at your unique competitive advantage. Clarify what elements you own (e.g., enabling technology). Consider whether it is worth filing patents and protecting your IP, and get professional advice in this area as required.

If your idea pits you against an established competitor, you must typically be "twice as good at half the cost." Customers don't switch away from a product or service they trust just because someone offers them an incrementally better deal.

Finally, don't underestimate your competition. Assume that they are as smart as you, and are constantly improving and working to build their advantage. They will not be standing by idly while someone else takes away their customers. The marketplace is constantly changing—while you are innovating, so is everyone else.

Tips for Gathering Competitive Intelligence

Market research is always helpful, especially when it comes to validating your advantage. If you can, talk with customers directly. Show actual quotes in your CO-STAR from people telling in their own words why they would choose your solution over other alternatives. Validating how they view the strengths and weaknesses of the competition can be very helpful as well, of course. Look beyond the current situation and consider the competitors that could threaten you both today and in the future.

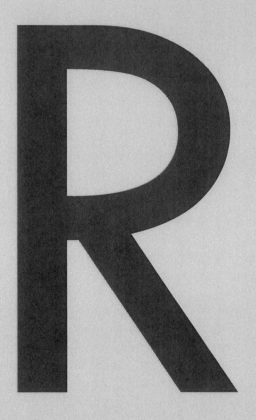

What results will be acheived?

What Results Will Be Achieved?

In the final section of your CO-STAR you identify and estimate the results that will be achieved from your solution, given the investment required and the costs incurred. Specifically, your task is to articulate the quantifiable rewards to the customer and the returns to your enterprise or funders. Clarify how all the key stakeholders benefit in tangible as well as intangible ways.

Rewards to Customers

Begin by describing the expected costs and investments required for your idea. Then list the customer or end-user benefits. Don't describe the features your solution delivers, but rather describe the rewards your customers will receive.

* List and quantify three to four major rewards that can be expected from your solution. If you don't yet have actual data, use the best realistic estimate you can generate. You can refine your projections over time with more research.
* It may help to distinguish buyers from end-customers or users. Are the rewards for each group different?
* Consider functional as well as aesthetic and emotional rewards: e.g., performance, design, reliability, ease of use, speed, simplicity, access, weight, cost, safety, compatibility, image, "love-ability," enjoyment, and belonging.

Returns to Funders

Identify returns to the enterprise or funders. Hopefully your analysis will allow you to provide a summary of financial projections that show you can achieve a level of success that far exceeds the necessary capital required. If not, you may have to rethink your solution. The types of measures you might consider are return on investment (ROI), profits, time to revenue, market share, reach, revenue growth, product leadership, and strategic fit. For example:

* Consider who specifically realizes the intended benefits. Do some stakeholders gain more than others? Earlier than others?
* Clarify the risks and show how these will be minimized and mitigated.
* Show the projections for key drivers of revenue, e.g., number of customers or units shipped.
* Give an estimated timeline for projected profit. When will investors expect to see a return on their investment, and how much profit would they expect to see?
* Will there be additional beneficial returns for funders and other stakeholders? Will there be gains in visibility? Increased positive feelings about the brand? Networking opportunities and relationship building? Recognition for leadership?

Ask yourself if the benefits are big enough that a buyer or customer would change their behavior and brand allegiance to purchase or use your solution. Are the returns big enough that funders would be delighted to invest in your solution?

Risk and Rewards

The "R" section of your value proposition is where you should also identify potential risks and think through how you will mitigate them. Consider market risks, technical risks, financial risks, risks from partners or suppliers, or any others that apply to your solution. Ensure your solution effectively minimizes each kind of risk.

⭐ Tips

* Present the results from the customer's point of view. For example, rather than say, "We ship in three to five days," you could say, "The product will typically arrive at the customer's door in three to five days."
* When quantifying results, the use of a common financial denominator (e.g., benefits per dollar) can assist with comparisons among multiple dimensions.
* In order to make projections about the potential profitability of your solution you need to establish a price. However, coming up with a price for a product that's never existed before can be tricky. Industry comparisons may offer you some insights, but one quick suggestion is to ask people in the target demographic for their opinion and feedback (e.g., What would you be willing to pay for ABC if it provided XYZ benefits?).

Sample
CO-STARs

4.

Sample CO-STARs

The following value propositions offer real-life examples of winning CO-STARs. Each is a novel response to the digital revolution and its potential to enrich and enable basic human activities—reading, shopping, and staying in touch. Several colleagues and clients have generously shared their work in progress, to show the practical and creative sides of real CO-STARs in action.

While each of these samples provides helpful insights into developing a high potential solution, they were selected as a group to demonstrate how CO-STARs can be used to champion a variety of solutions for distinct customers with diverse needs.

These three CO-STARs illustrate a wide range of types of innovation:

* Idea Generators: Who Created the CO-STARs—Innovators working inside companies or entrepreneurs starting new companies.
* Levels of Maturity of the CO-STARs: Early-stage thinking or more advanced concepts.
* Writing Styles: Short bullets or paragraphs and prose.
* Proof Points: Scenarios and quantified research.
* Market Segments: From teenage gamers to older residents in senior living homes.
* Technology Strategies: Increasing features versus simplifying functionality.
* Impacted Sectors: Private and public.
* Commercial Relationships: Consumer-oriented or business to business.

As you will discover from these examples, there is no one right way to draft a value proposition. All six questions in CO-STAR should be answered and quantification is a must, but you can choose how to develop your initial CO-STARs to best suit your style, your particular project, and your audience.

Sample CO-STAR #1: Egmont Publishing's Young Adult Transmedia Story

CO-STAR has been the centrepiece of Egmont Publishing's innovation efforts around the globe. The Kids Media division of Egmont International was willing to share the following outline from an early draft of one of their winning CO-STARs—for a Young Adult Transmedia Story. This CO-STAR is one of many terrific ideas that have been successfully developed, pitched, approved, and produced by Egmont's global workforce.

"Over 3 years ago we introduced an innovation challenge to encourage more ideas to develop our business. The results have been impressive at multiple levels:
* **Common practices and tools across the 24 countries in our division.**
* **Importing and exporting ideas across the division.**
* **Creating a more entrepreneurial spirit and learning from mistakes.**
* **Enhancing the skills and experience of our staff—we have trained innovators, facilitators and idea generators who have developed their ideas.**
* **Innovation played its part in contributing cost efficiency ideas which lead to over €23m savings across the division."**

Dawn Cordy, Innovation Director, Egmont Kids Media

An Early CO-STAR: A Young Adult Transmedia Story

Customer

Our customers and their interests:

12–13 years old: Looking to older siblings for what's cool; waiting for independence.

14–18 years old: Author's core fans; rebellious and focused on self-discovery; key consumers for web aspect of digital story and game.

18–24 years old: Have an emerging sense of responsibility; key consumer for IOS/Android app game.

Opportunity

To take the story to where the digitally fluent audience is, rather than relying on them to find the book through traditional routes (retailers and libraries).

To have a direct relationship with consumers and allow them to participate in the action.

To learn about the skills required for transmedia publishing and new business models.

Solution

A brilliantly written story that starts as an Alternative Reality Game (ARG), evolves through social media and an app, and finally culminates in a book. Chapter One of the book takes off where the ARG and digital story ends.

Team

The author: Writer and creator.

The digital production team: Responsible for the story and game as it plays out across social media and the app, including management of the community.

Egmont Press: Book publisher responsible for the editorial and print publishing worldwide. Also the investor.

Advantage

We learned from other publishing digital ventures and alternative reality games and applied a few key lessons to give us advantages over competing offerings:

* Our transmedia story will be translatable so that foreign publishers can buy into key elements of the digital piece.

* Each element—digital and print—will be a satisfying gaming or reading experience in its own right, so that consumers can jump in at any point and not have to buy into the whole transmedia piece. At the same time, each element must be part of a seamless story arc, coherent and satisfying for those who want the whole transmedia experience.

* The story is king: The digital piece will only be as good as the writing, so we must invest in a top writer with a strong sales track record and fan base.

Results

Rewards for customers

* A story brought to them, in their space, using their social media and their devices.
* A story that allows them to participate.
* A brilliant, edge-of-your-seat thriller from a bestselling author at the top of his game.

Return for Egmont

Generate revenue while also gaining:
* Digital lessons (we'll learn more about how to deliver value in this new genre).
* Insight about our consumers.
* Building a following for our author.

Sample CO-STAR #2: Families in Touch

The inspiration for the company Families in Touch came from the personal experience of one of its founders, Steve Goddard. Steve had recently retired from his role as a senior executive in a leading multi-national engineering company. Within six months of his retirement, his father passed away and he needed to find a care home for his mother. In the course of viewing many different care homes, Steve spotted an unmet customer need—the need for older people (75 years+) to stay in touch with their families despite being unable to use a computer. He began working with a former supplier and colleague who was a computer programmer and with a young product designer. The three of them played with their idea for six months and developed a rough prototype. Then they went to Cida Co, an organization that offered training and coaching on innovation, entrepreneurial skills, and business development. Cida Co helped them turn their ideas into an effective CO-STAR value proposition for their new company.

Customer

Primary Customer:
Private sector residential/care homes seeking to achieve three-star accreditation by the UK government's Care Quality Commission (CQC) who are responsible for ensuring government standards are met in the provision of care.

Secondary Customer:
Elderly people currently or likely to become residents in care homes.
Families of those in care homes.

Unmet Need:
The ability to have real-time communication, both written and oral, with family members as often as required without the need to develop IT/computer literacy skills.

Opportunity

There are 20,819 care homes in the UK owned by 2,135 group homeowners. Even 10% of the higher-quality homes create a viable UK market. Estimated potential profit £500,000 in three years. However, clearly this need is experienced in care homes and among older people the world over, so there is the potential for a global market to build on UK success.

Additionally, the technology could be effectively used in other environments: e.g., working with disadvantaged young people; immigrant communities where English is not the first language.

Solution

The proposed solution is a social-networking portal for older people that uses an easy and versatile digital platform. This device would enable older people to feel less isolated from their loved ones as they would be able to receive and look at photos, videos, and email messages from family members no matter how far away they might be. It would enable the care home resident to access newspapers, photos, event listings, etc., local to their families so as to feel in touch with their relatives and their communities.

The integrated service comprises a touch-screen monitor supported by simplified photo, video, voicemail, and web conferencing. Email templates would be provided to enable residents to send notes and respond to emails and photos without the effort of learning to operate a keyboard. A keyboard can be provided for those able to use it. The application will be provided to the care home as a fully managed service, thus removing the need for IT expertise within the care home.

The primary sale would be to the high-end care home owners, who would need to take the leasing responsibility of the customized hardware. A basic service would be available to all residents.

A secondary sale would be to families who would be invited to subscribe, with the option of upgrading the basic service to one provided on a gold/silver/bronze price-rating system. It is anticipated that concerned families who aren't able to visit in person as often as they feel they should would drive the purchase of higher levels of service.

Over the next five to ten years, as the generations change and a more computer-literate generation becomes the resident population, the team will improve and update the communications services, with constant innovation provided to meet the needs and expectations of an increasingly technologically sophisticated customer base.

The marketing and sales effort would be critical. An early strategy based on "Seeing is Believing" would be adopted, so that both the care home personnel and the residents themselves could experience the benefits at first hand, on a trial basis. Word of mouth in a relatively small commercial world would be essential. Achieving and sustaining the high CQC rating is the objective of the most expensive of the commercial care homes and, for a while at least, this could provide genuine competitive advantage.

Team

* The three co-founders of the company:
  ◉ Steve Goddard—IT director level, worked for £16.3 billion company—global infrastructure—director of 160 projects worldwide. Established a 250-seat software development centre in Malaysia. Would have primary responsibility for sales.
  ◉ Mark McEvoy—software expert with his own successful software development company. Would have primary responsibility for software development and management.
  ◉ Ritch Partridge—graphic artist and product designer, owns his own company; would have primary responsibility for GUI design, user experience and product appeal.

* Independent technical architect—the founders want an independent perspective with a commitment to continuing innovation.
* Market research and strategy specialist, to work closely with Steve on supporting sales strategy.

Advantage

* Technology that is simple and beautiful, that is not daunting in any way.
* Provides easy access to communications even for the most technophobic elderly person, requiring no new skills or knowledge, and provides individual and private communications.
* Offers families a unique way of staying in touch; benefits are scaled according to family subscription—gold, silver, and bronze.
* Easy to install and manage, excellent service back-up.
* Constant innovation as a key characteristic of the company service.

Results

* Significantly increased chances of participating care homes receiving/sustaining highest standard of CQC recommendation on "quality of life" criterion.
* Improved relationships between care homes and family customers.
* In 20% of three-star CQC care homes in the UK in three years; in 40% of three-star CQC homes in five years.
* £500,000 net profit in three years.

Conclusion

Founder Steve Goddard commented: **"The use of the CO-STAR methodology was a godsend for us. Until we met Cida Co, we had been playing at the edges, not making the commitment needed to turn a bright idea into a business. Making us go through the CO-STAR process made us look at everything, question everything, evaluate everything. It made us realize both the potential of the idea and the seriousness required if** we were to bring the idea to market. Eighteen months later, we have a product and interested customers; we have a marketing strategy in place; and we are three months away from the launch. We know we would never have gone on this journey without the work we did with Cida Co using CO-STAR."

Sample CO-STAR #3: Sustainable Shopper

Contributed by Roger Kirby, an innovation champion from Swisscom, in Switzerland

Customer

"Current global consumption patterns are unsustainable... It is becoming apparent that efficiency gains and technological advances alone will not be sufficient to bring global consumption to a sustainable level; changes will also be required to consumer lifestyles, including the ways in which consumers choose and use products and services."

—*Sustainable Consumption Facts & Trends, World Business Council for Sustainable Development*

There is growing concern among consumers about sustainability (e.g., 96% of Europeans report that protecting the environment is a priority). However, for consumers to turn this concern into purchases is difficult. There is not enough information about where to find sustainable products and services. Changing the shopping behavior of consumers means making the discovery and sharing of sustainable products and services convenient and fun.

Opportunity

Social shopping, the integration of social networks with retail commerce, is growing rapidly. We see this in the power of the Facebook community to affect the reputation of brands, the popularity of sites such as www.groupon.com for daily deals, and the ability to use the mobile phone to access product information and compare prices. Consumers are reviewing and rating products and places on sites such as www.epinions.com and www.likelist.com, among many others.

Hyper-location services on mobile phones are enhancing social shopping by enabling people to discover great products and places in their immediate vicinity (e.g., www.facebook.com/deals and eBay's acquisition of Where).

Combining these capabilities will revolutionize how consumers decide what to buy and how retailers attract customers. Today these technologies can support consumers concerned with sustainability issues such as fair trade, environment, waste, and renewable energy: the "Sustainable Shoppers."

We estimate that we can help two million consumers within four years, turning them into Sustainable Shoppers through their iPhones and Android handsets.

Solution

How it works: The story of Dan, a consumer concerned about sustainability.

Dan goes out of his way to find products that come from suppliers who respect the rights and well-being of everyone along their supply chain. He also prefers products that are manufactured with responsible use of resources and energy.

1. The Sustainable Shopper application on Dan's iPhone shows him where to find products that meet his high standards. He can search and find the location of products in any geographic area he chooses or be alerted to the shops nearby that may carry what he wants.
2. When Dan finds an unfamiliar product on the shelf, he takes a quick snapshot of the 1D barcode, printed on nearly all packages, and instantly receives information about the product from the Sustainable online community.
3. When he buys the product, he presses a button that checks it into the Sustainable community, adding Sustainability Points to the product's score.
- Once a product receives sufficient Points through purchases by community members, it is eligible for the Sustainable Label, which can be printed on packaging and used in advertising.
4. At the same time, Dan's own score as a Sustainable Shopper is increased. If he wishes, he can also publish what he has purchased on his community profile, rate the product and write a review.
- The points that Dan accumulates are redeemable for discounts on Sustainable Label products.

5. Meanwhile, his GPS position is used to identify the shop where he made the purchase and automatically check-in Dan at that location. The shop is assigned points toward its own Sustainable rating.

- A store that accumulates enough Points also receives a Sustainable Label that it can display on the premises and use in advertising.

6. Dan is participating in a growing community of consumers who can act on their concerns about the environment, energy, free trade, and sustainability through informed purchases. Their influence becomes a powerful incentive for stores and product manufacturers to provide sustainable goods and services.

Team

The Sustainable Shopper service will be developed by a core team with experience in mobile marketing and social networks. We also have access to experts in sustainable products at key universities and nonprofit organizations.

We will partner with leading startups to complete our skill set and implement our service online and on Apple and Android mobile devices. We have identified potential partners for the following:

* Barcode reading on the mobile handset with interfaces top product databases because we will need high-quality, high-speed barcode reading capability, analytics for products being scanned, location of scans, information about products and support of barcodes most often used (e.g., EAN8, UPC-E, UPC12, EAN13, Code39, Code128).

* Access to product databases with high volume of items

* (40,000+). Our panel of independent sustainability experts will rate an initial set of 5,000 to trigger reviews by the online community.

* Mapping system for geo-location and routing on mobile device, which will enable users to find stores with sustainable products.

Advantage

* The Sustainable Label is created by the community. This removes the confusion created by a multitude of Green labels currently on the market. Consumers will purchase products with the Sustainable Label because they trust the reviews and recommendations of other consumers. The shops and products rewarded with the label will benefit from viral marketing.
* Shoppers can easily find products and services that they consider to be sustainable.
* Shoppers will receive discounts as rewards for purchasing key products and services.
* Products and shops granted the Sustainable Label can send targeted advertising to community members based on purchasing profiles and interests they have expressed to the online community.
* Revenue is generated for us through targeted advertising.
* We also take a small percentage of revenue from the sale of products that have achieved sufficient popularity to receive the Sustainable Label.
  Many "social" and "location-based" shopping services are appearing on the market but few meet an important need for consumers. Sustainable Shopper combines the best capabilities in hyper-location, social networking, and product data to enable consumers to locate products and services that are often difficult to discover. The simple and convenient

approach of Sustainable Shopper reduces this work to nearly nothing, making finding and sharing sustainable goods a natural part of modern shopping. Our business and technical ecosystem also ensures the highest quality of service. The model we are building will be integrated within the next two years into mobile payment services.

Results

- We expect costs for development, licenses of technology and cloud services of $450,000 in the first two years.
- After four years, we anticipate two million community members who use our service on mobile devices, riding a wave of growing consumer concern and increased availability of sustainable products.
- We expect advertising revenue of $10.5 million by year four.

Perfect Pitching: Getting to "Yes!"

5.

Perfect Pitching: Getting to "Yes!"

Life's a Pitch!

Like the majority of ideas, yours will most likely begin in quite an unfinished form. Don't let that stop you. Many "big ideas" start that way. They become a success through relentless testing, regular exchanges with others, getting feedback and improving the idea continuously, until it finally finds its full potential. To achieve this result you must be able to talk effectively about your idea, get others interested in it, integrate their feedback, and ask for their help. Pitching your idea, whether it's to your boss, a partner, or a VC, is an essential innovation skill. Once you have researched and written your CO-STAR, the time will come when you will need to talk about your idea in order to take your thinking to the next level or to gain approval. Some methods of pitching are:

* The "elevator pitch" is a short (one to three minute) persuasive summary of your value proposition. The goal is to garner interest in your idea and set up a longer follow-up session where you can provide more details. The analogy is a movie preview that gets a potential viewer interested in seeing the film when it's released. You never know when an opportunity to share your idea might arise. Be prepared to give your pitch at any time. Elevator pitches can open doors to new possibilities, and are the equivalent of a resume for a job hunt.
* The "developmental pitch" is typically offered to friends, colleagues, and subject matter experts. The goal is to test and improve your idea through constructive dialogue and suggestions from the audience.

* The "sales pitch" is used to close the deal. You are looking for approval and some investment of resources from decision-makers. These tend to be formal meetings requiring a sound business case, a well-defined plan, and a promising ROI.

Many people believe that they can present their ideas "off the cuff," with a minimum of planning or thought. But in practice, few people are that gifted. There are a number of benefits to the well-planned pitch:

- You will be able to concentrate on the delivery of the presentation.
- You will not have to search for words to persuade people—they will come naturally in the most logical order.
- You will have tailored key messages to the interest of the audience.

Crafting your idea may be more important than the idea itself. What good is an idea, if no one is interested in it?

Structure: Hook, Highlights, Request

While each pitch is different in length and emphasis, they are all based on CO-STAR and share a similar underlying structure. An effective pitch contains three key components:

1. The hook: You want to get your listener's attention with a short, compelling summary statement that demon-strates to them that you have a unique solution to a relevant problem. A typical starting point is a question or statement such as: "What if...?" or "Imagine if..." or "Eighty million people today suffer from..." (numbers are always compelling!), followed by a single-sentence claim about what you have in mind to deal with the problem.

2. **The highlights:** Select the relevant elements from your CO-STAR value proposition. This is the description of the problem and the opportunity, of the unique solution your team can deliver, and of the results that can be expected from your solution that far surpass the alternatives.

3. **The request:** Conclude your pitch with a request—a next step. Be clear in your mind how your listeners can help you realize your idea, then ask for their support. Do you need a longer meeting to discuss your value proposition in more detail? Support for building a prototype or a full business plan? Authorization for research? Money? Time? People? Introductions to others? Sometimes innovators get so caught up in delivering a good pitch that they forget the whole reason they were pitching in the first place. Remember what you want and why you are pitching.

What Makes a Good Hook?

A good hook is simple, yet engages the listener quickly. It introduces an important problem to be solved, with a bit of emotional charge attached. It will make your audience want your solution, even before you present it. Some examples of strong hooks we have heard include:

* "Would you like to live longer?" This opening line quickly pulled in audience attention for a digital device that would help users track their individual exercise and nutrition.
* "Imagine you are walking through a crowd with your three-year-old daughter. She was holding your hand one minute, but the next, she is gone. You look through the crowd, but don't see her anywhere. Where could she be? What can you do?"
Painting this chilling scenario helped make the case for selling GPS bracelets for toddlers to concerned parents.

⭐ Tips for Pitching Your CO-STAR

* Talk directly to your audience—never read your slides! It's important to know your pitch inside out, so you can take the time to connect with your audience, rather than look to your slides for the next point. This will also make you more relaxed if someone asks a question that you think needs to be answered.

* Customize your pitch to the given situation and to your audience:
  ◉ Know your audience and focus your pitch on the content they would most want to hear. Show them what is important to them (e.g., VCs want to know the ROI; customers want to know what they can do with your new product or service).
  ◉ Introduce trust-building points when you can (e.g., mention the name of someone they respect who has endorsed your idea).
  ◉ If you are pitching to a potential customer, your value proposition must be compelling and differentiated. To be compelling it needs to hit the hotspots of your targeted customers in their language. To be differentiated it needs to clearly state how your offering is better than your competitors' around the elements that are the most important to your customers.

* All presentations are a type of theater, so tell an easy-to-repeat story about your idea or offer anecdotes to help illustrate key points. It all helps to make your presentation more effective and memorable.

Use metaphors and analogies to:
◉ Bring added texture to the presentation
◉ Make a point
◉ Help the complex and unknown feel more familiar
◉ Make your pitch memorable.

* Offer facts and figures – quantitative information is persuasive. If you have no specific data yet, start with a realistic "best guess."

* Show a diagram, display mock-ups, or even do a skit to bring your idea to life.

Remember, less is more:

There is an old saying that, "No one ever complained about a presentation being too short." Nothing kills a presentation more than going on too long.

With an elevator pitch you are aiming to give just enough information to get people curious, gather their feedback, and get them to want more. Keep it to less than three minutes if you can.

When you are making a developmental pitch or sales pitch where you are expected to use slides and provide more detail, follow Guy Kawasaki's (2004) 10—20—30 rule: 10 slides, 20 minutes, and 30-point font.

* Pick a time and place where your audience won't be distracted. Even if you know the venue, take the time to check out the presentation room. Arrive early and make sure that the audio and video are working. Work out where you will need to stand.

* Be relaxed, but show your passion. Confidence can be contagious, so speak clearly and enthusiastically.

* Practice makes for perfect performance. Rehearsal is the biggest single thing that you can do to improve your performance. Perform your presentation out loud at least three to five times, especially if it is a sales pitch. Practice, but avoid becoming a "canned salesperson."

* Start and end on time. It shows respect for the audience and demonstrates your professionalism.

* Be gracious and thankful for all feedback and suggestions. Even if you don't close the deal, it is important to maintain positive relationships with your innovation ecosystem.

* Video yourself: Set up a video camera and record yourself making the pitch. You will see all sorts of mistakes that you are making, from lowering your voice during the sections where you are less confident, to talking to your slides rather than the audience, to how often you say "like."

* Have a back-up plan. Be prepared just in case the technology doesn't work in the room where you are presenting:
  - In addition to a laptop with your presentation, take a printed set of slides.
  - Take a memory stick with your presentation on it.
  - If you can, take along small portable speakers if your presentation includes video or audio that you want to ensure your audience will hear.

* Watch out for MEGO: "My Eyes Glaze Over." This is a troubling condition that can afflict audiences when a presenter uses too much jargon, gets too technical, or starts reading from the slides. Try to aim your pitch for maximum audience engagement.

The existential mantra for innovators:

I pitch, therefore I am.

Your
One-line
CO-STAR

6.
Your One-Line CO-STAR

So What Are You Working On?

Imagine you are at a networking reception and a person who has the resources to help your project asks, "So what are you working on?" Or imagine if you actually do meet a person in the prototypical elevator who could fund your project, but you are only going to the fourth floor—how can you give a very brief one-liner that generates enough interest that you are invited for a longer conversation?

For these occasions, it is good to have a one-line CO-STAR ready. Pick the most compelling elements of your proposition and create an easy-to-recall statement that will capture the interest of your audience.

To get started you might fill in the blanks below:

Our _____ will enable _____
       (solution)   (customer)
to _____ better than _____.
  (get specific results)   (the competition)

For example:

Our <u>cloud computing security solution</u> not only <u>protects sensitive corporate data</u> from <u>malware</u> but also <u>detects and prevents attacks from hackers and thieves 60%</u> better than <u>traditional encryption methods.</u>

Or you might try:

I am working with _____ on a _____
                    (team)   (solution)
that will _____.
          (opportunity)

For example:

I am working with <u>the Olympic team</u> on <u>high-performance racing attire</u> that will <u>bring a whole new line of clothing to the billion-dollar ski apparel industry.</u>

Getting Smart *Fast:* Improving Your CO-STAR

7.
Getting Smart Fast: Improving Your CO-STAR

An important phase that too often is left out of the innovation process is the "value improvement phase." Sometimes, innovators and entrepreneurs come up with a great idea, develop a value proposition and a pitch, and then assume they are ready to pitch for project acceptance or funding. In fact, ideas are rarely at their best at the very beginning.

In a globally competitive world, your finished value proposition must be as strong as possible. You want your idea to grow up, to develop its full potential. Yet, in today's dynamic business (and social and cultural) environment, almost no one has the expertise in every area needed to develop a strong CO-STAR value proposition. Gathering collective intelligence from others becomes essential.

The value improvement phase is the time when innovators take their CO-STAR out into the world; deliver their pitch to people who can give them helpful feedback; consider the feedback carefully; and refine their CO-STAR. The most successful innovators and entrepreneurs are not shy about sharing their ideas. They understand that it's the only way to get better.

CO-STAR as a Tool for Feedback

One of the reasons it is helpful for innovators to have a simple and shared tool for value propositions is that it enables clear feedback from others. CO-STAR enables colleagues, advisors, content experts, and even friends and family to do much more than simply tell you whether they liked your pitch or not. It gives individuals hearing your pitch an easy way to organize their feedback to you. Too often, feedback is not really helpful. Colleagues and friends may judge your idea, tell you whether they like it or not, but they rarely tell you how you could make your idea stronger. You may hear responses such as, "That will never work," or, "Yeah, I like it! I would buy that!" But you may not discover precisely what makes them think your solution would not work or even what they liked most.

By using CO-STAR as a feedback tool, your listeners can give you focused input: Do they have new ideas for you about your Customer, Opportunity, Solution, Team, Advantage, or Result? Is there a specific area they don't understand? Do they have an idea about how you could make that specific element stronger? Do they know others who could be helpful to you in any of these areas?

"We find that innovative products really are the product of many minds. A very small team might drive the initial design and creation of the concept, but having multiple people look at, evaluate, comment on, and lend supporting insights is valuable. The trick is to allow these additional insights to be supportive, and not weigh the original ideas down with extraneous freight."

Dan Russell, research scientist and search anthropologist, Google

Running a Rapid Idea Improvement Session (RIIS)

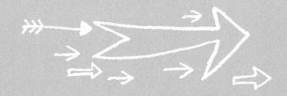

8.

Running a Rapid Idea Improvement Session (RIIS)

One very effective way for people to co-develop breakthrough innovations is by convening a Rapid Idea Improvement Session (RIIS). Activities at RIIS sessions include practicing pitches, sharing prototypes, and obtaining feedback to create compelling CO-STAR value propositions. A RIIS can be a casual meeting, where you supply food and drinks and invite interested colleagues to help you develop your value proposition and your pitch. A RIIS can also be a formal part of a work setting, where you invite individuals who could add valuable expertise and perspective to your idea. You can even include customers in a RIIS session to help you build a solution that really does meet their needs; to help you create a solution your customers will love.

RIIS sessions provide a way to rapidly test and iterate concepts, gather diverse perspectives, and help innovators and their teams develop their ideas. Presentations at RIIS sessions are short, typically follow the CO-STAR format, and become increasingly quantitative and detailed as they mature. Participants at RIIS sessions provide feedback with specific suggestions to enhance the value of ideas presented.

Point of View: Feedback is Golden

RIIS sessions come along with a mindset—that feedback is golden. When people take time to give you input and new information you might not have had otherwise, it is a valuable gift. Therefore, if you have a room full of people and a half-hour of their time, you do NOT want to present for 25 minutes, leave 5 minutes for feedback at the end, and then defend yourself against any changes your audience members suggest by telling them how you already thought about that beforehand. Instead, you should present for 5 minutes, and gather feedback for 25 minutes, gleaning every bit of information and support you can.

Learning to Listen to Feedback: An Exercise

For many innovators, it is not easy to listen to feedback. When you present your CO-STAR pitch for feedback, try this exercise: Don't respond as participants give you their feedback, or get pulled into conversations about whether their comments make sense. Just listen, take in what they are telling you, and then thank them for their thoughts.

From running workshops and training sessions with innovators across many fields, we have discovered an interesting pattern. When novice innovators know they can respond to participants' feedback, something happens to the innovators that blocks out learning. They start thinking while listening to the feedback, and too often, the "background conversation" inside the innovator's head is all about how to convince the audience that the issue being addressed is not really a problem. Instead of listening to the feedback, taking it in, and learning from it, the innovator is planning what to say to justify the CO-STAR as it is. They try to win, rather than learn. So, while it seems quite unnatural to have an innovator present his or her CO-STAR, and then only listen to feedback and not respond at all, it is a great learning experience.

Once innovators have tried this exercise several times, they find it easier to actually listen and take in the feedback from RIIS sessions. Then it is "safe" to return to a more typical back-and-forth exchange between participants and presenters without jeopardizing the whole reason for the RIIS—learning. Remember, in the value improvement phase, your goals are to learn and to make your pitch as good as possible.

Types of RIIS Sessions

RIIS sessions can be used for:

* A single presenter who offers an in-depth pitch and gathers feedback from participants.
* Multiple presenters, where team members for one CO-STAR value proposition give feedback to presenters for the other value propositions.
* A company or organization, where a group may meet regularly around a particular theme. (E.g., once-a-month RIIS sessions focused on "Green Products and Services," or "Engaging Our Customers Through Social Media," or "Improving Customer Experience.")

RIIS sessions can be face to face, by teleconference or web conference, or online (See Q+ discussion, Chapter 10).

Who Attends a RIIS, and What Are Their Roles?

Facilitator

* Opens the event with welcome and introductions, frames the event (e.g., "we're here to learn"), and reviews timing.
* Organizes the timeline. For example, in a 90-minute RIIS, with 3 innovation teams presenting, each innovation team gets 30 minutes, which includes their time to set up. Sets expectations

minutes assigned to set up and take down, with 5 minutes to present, and 20 minutes for feedback.

* Helps presenters stick to their timeline with signs or signals to alert them when their time is almost up.
* Ensures that presenters know to listen openly and that participants know to give feedback.
* Gently coaches presenters and participants as required. It takes time for people to learn the culture of a RIIS, to learn that it is about discovery, improvement, and a commitment to value.

Champion/Innovator

* Selects and invites people to the session.
* Prepares themself and their CO-STAR for the session
* Sets up and runs the RIIS, if there is not a facilitator present.
* Presents the CO-STAR quickly—then listens to feedback.
* Collects input from all the attendees, and listens non-defensively.
* After the RIIS, integrates feedback and improves their CO-STAR.
* If significant changes have been made to the CO-STAR based on the feedback received, the champion/innovator may want to invite the same group back again to respond to the updated version. Has the feedback been interpreted correctly? Has the CO-STAR moved in the direction they hoped?

Team Members Who Are Not Presenting

* Listen and take notes.
* Capture all the details in the feedback, so it can be used to improve the value proposition.
* If someone's feedback is unclear, asks clarifying questions, but watches out for the slippery slope of trying to defend the team's value proposition. These questions should simply

help the team to thoroughly understand participant's feedback, not to change their minds.

Participant Giving Feedback

* Gives focused and specific feedback around each of the CO-STAR sections (C, O, S, T, A, and R).
* If asked to respond as a Fan or a Builder, does that first. Additional comments can always be given in the All Play section of the RIIS.

Gathering Feedback

We have found that gathering focused and specific input in three waves is most useful for quickly enhancing your value proposition. Consider feedback from the perspective of:

* Fans: Appreciative feedback, identifying the existing strengths of the pitch.
* Builders: Constructive feedback, identifying ways to make the pitch stronger.
* Customers: User or buyer insights (participants role play when no customers are present).

Before each pitch, assign two or three listeners to each role, so that participants listen to each pitch from the designated perspective. Ask two or three people to take the role of a Fan, two or three others to take the role of a Builder, and another two or three to be Customers. After the pitch, Fans give their feedback first, so presenters get to hear what is already great about their pitch. This helps presenters hear the later suggestions about how their pitch can become stronger and lays a foundation for the work ahead.

If you are not pitching to an actual customer group, assign each participant giving customer feedback to roleplay a particular kind of customer. E.g., for the pitch of a GPS device for cars to be marketed to concerned parents of teenage drivers, where the device tracks the speed and location of the vehicle and sends it back to the owner's website, one participant could be asked to play a 17-year-old girl who drives her parents' car, and another participant could be the girl's father who is the owner of the car. Each "customer" would then listen to your pitch and give feedback from that unique perspective.

Giving SMART Feedback

Anyone who frequently reads comments on blogs or news sites knows that feedback covers a wide range of helpfulness, to put it mildly. People often use feedback as a chance to release anger and frustration. Or sometimes they try to kill ideas with comments that basically say, "That will never work," or "That's impossible," without saying why or what might help.

In contrast, we encourage participants to give SMART feedback:

* Specific: Vague generalities are not that helpful. Be as specific as possible: "I found your Results section to be quite compelling because of X, Y, Z."
* Maximizing: Build, strengthen, and expand the idea to its full potential: "You may be able to double your projections if you include…"
* Actionable: Suggest steps the innovator could take to improve content and presentation: "If you add companies X and Y to your list of competitors, you will have captured all the big players."
* Respectful: Act like a friend. Be honest and caring. Honor the

efforts of the presenter: "The Opportunity was clearer in this version of your COSTAR, and could be even stronger if you could further segment the audience into..."
* Timely: Be brief. Keep your feedback to the point and avoid long speeches: "I've made my point. Let me send you the report I mentioned and you can see if the findings align with yours."

After the CO-STAR Pitch: Questions for Participants

For Fans:

* What do you love about the idea?
* What was most moving or memorable and why?
* What was most convincing?
* When giving the pitch again, what should we keep the same?
* What should be emphasized in any future pitch?

For Builders:

* How can we optimize our idea and construct a stronger CO-STAR?
* What would make this idea stronger?
* Where could we improve the value of this idea?
* When giving this pitch again, what should we add or leave out of the pitch?
* Was there any part of the pitch you didn't understand? If so, what would make it clearer for you?
* Do you know of people or resources that could further enhance this idea?

For Customers:

Customers should stay in role and respond, "I liked your idea because ____, and it would be stronger if ____."

All Play:

Once Fans, Builders, and Customers have given feedback, any participant can comment from any perspective in the "All Play" section of the RIIS.

Participants should organize their comments around CO-STAR. For example:

* "I really liked the way your hook made me feel the intensity of the problem your customers have."
* "I liked the way your diagrams showed the size of the opportunity. Very convincing."
* "I think your customers would also be worried about..."
* "I would like to see a breakdown of your customers by age group."
* "Given that your target customer group is women, I'd like to see more women on your team."
* "I just downloaded an app for $4.99 that does a lot of what you are suggesting."
* Or, on very good days for innovators, "I have a friend at XYZ company who has been looking for a solution just like this."

 ## Tips

* If you present your CO-STAR and people tell you something they wished they had heard, and you actually have that information but left it out of the presentation on purpose, just be aware that your audience missed it. It doesn't help to defend yourself by trying to explain why you left it out. You only need to learn that people wanted to hear it. If this is a

consistent message, consider whether you need to put the information back in.

* Thank everyone for feedback at the end of the RIIS session, and offer a way for people to stay connected to your project if they are interested.

* As a participant in a RIIS, when giving feedback, be honest AND respectful. Imagine that this person may later be a participant in a RIIS where you are pitching. Help innovators to improve their ideas while keeping their spirit of innovation alive.

* Innovation champions and teams need to take in the implications of feedback, which are sometimes quite serious. Do they need to recruit help to get essential skills their team is lacking? Should they double their efforts to race against competitors trying to get their solution to market first? Or should they re-define their idea or give it up altogether? There are many times when an innovator recognizes that one idea won't work, only to wake up at 3:00 a.m. the next morning with a clear view of a new approach to the solution that could actually succeed.

Prototyping: Making It Real

9.
Prototyping: Making It Real

Rapid prototyping is a powerful tool for making your solution real. It makes abstract ideas tangible and facilitates further exploration of your proposed solution. It is enormously valuable to be able to see, touch, and experience the end state. Prototyping is about "learning through doing" and is one of the ways you can educate yourself as efficiently as possible to see if your idea is a good fit with target customers and market.

Innovation is in many ways like a puzzle. There are certain best practices associated with innovation, similar to "turn over all the pieces" and "start with the edges," but at the end of the day puzzling requires lots of trial and error. No one thinks their way through a jigsaw puzzle!

Prototyping is about unleashing the spirit of experimentation: Coming up with ideas is important, but testing out your ideas in an engaging and visual manner with colleagues and customers often adds something very special. We use the term "rapid prototyping" in the broadest sense, which includes:

- **Pictures, sketches and diagrams of your solution**
- **Mock-ups**
- **Working prototypes**
- **Enactments.**

You don't have to be an architect, engineer or artist; anyone can be a rapid prototyper. Just go back in time and recall all the fun and creativity you brought to all those school projects as a kid. Gather magazines, wood, wire, foam, cardboard, paint, glue, duct tape, etc., and start building. If you are more comfortable with a digital toolkit, use your computer to create visuals of your idea. You don't need vast sums of money to prototype, just some ingenuity.

By bringing your idea into the physical world you make it real and give it momentum. Benefits to rapid prototyping include:

* Innovators and entrepreneurs learn from building, experimenting, testing, tweaking, and generally coming up with cost-effective ways to identify potential failure points.
* Customers and colleagues provide illumination into areas of clarity and confusion, pleasant surprises (e.g., unexpected benefits), and causes for concern; counterintuitive insights; and alternatives and new opportunities.
* Sponsors get enhanced understanding of the idea and an early demonstration of desirability and feasibility.

Pictures

Pictures add to your value proposition by helping your audience to visualize a problem or opportunity, or more clearly understand your solution and how it would appear in practice. We have all heard the old adage, "A picture is worth a thousand words." In some cases it is worth a billion dollars. Future CEO Herb Kelleher drew a triangle on the back of a cocktail napkin connecting Dallas, San Antonio, and Houston to help explain his plan to his partners. This diagram was the launching point for Southwest Airlines, one of the most successful carriers in the world.

★ Tips

* Begin by creating an outline of your idea and then slowly adding in the details.
* Don't waste time on details that aren't necessary: Think about what elements should be highlighted and what things aren't important or should be downplayed.
* You don't have to achieve perfection on the first shot. Redraw things or move features around to get a better illustration. Use a pencil and white paper so you can easily erase and refine your sketch or use one of the many drawing or presentation software tools to create an image of your idea.
* In addition to creating a picture of your idea it can be helpful to sketch your proposed business model (e.g., indicate all the key players and how they relate to one another to track the flow of goods and money).

Mock-ups

A mock-up is an early stage, very basic model of your idea. It offers a 3D tangible rendering that highlights the core elements of your solution. Mock-ups offer early insights at low cost with minimal emotional attachments because they can be easily changed.

★ Tips

* Be creative and cost-efficient: Build your mock-up from office supplies and/or everyday objects (cardboard, tape, wire, foam, magazine pictures, Lego, wood, etc.).
* Be relevant: Highlight the most important features.
* Be forgiving: Don't be a perfectionist, "quick and dirty" will be fine for the first pass.

* Be visual: If you can't build it, draw it (see tips in picture section).
* Be playful: Use your imagination and have fun.

Prototypes

Prototypes add a functional element and are good for testing the tricky parts, cheaply. Instead of only getting feedback from others about whether they guess customers would like or use your product, you can try out an early prototype with real customers and find out how they respond to it.

 ## Tips

* Mock-up plus: Apply guidelines from mock-ups.
* Clear intent: Prototype with specific goals in mind (e.g., get answers to the "big" questions and feedback on the riskiest elements).
* Mix and match: Blending high and low tech is OK.
* Peel the onion: Test different solutions to same problem.
* Build a dependable demo: Practice and refine until your prototype works (limited functionality should still function!).

Enactments

For innovators who work with a team or who are fortunate enough to have access to supportive colleagues, skits and role playing are great for demonstrating prototypes in practice. They are especially useful for exploring new services and business processes. Invite other people to participate or view your proposed solution in context by enacting an integrated customer experience.

★ Tips

* Get into the role: Don't tell the audience about the idea—stay in role and act it out.
* Use props: Try and recreate key elements of the environment you will be replicating, but remember you can always act out new situations and technologies. Incorporate your mock-ups/prototypes.
* Invent whole experiences: Consider staging (the beginning, middle, and end) as well as the key elements (technology, space, or people) when developing scenarios.
* Rehearse and learn: The team should practice the skit. Test ideas by acting out key interactions. Try them out, then stop and reflect on what is and isn't working.
* Stay focused: It is tempting to come up with elaborate scenarios, so make sure the proper time and attention is given to the most significant parts of your ideas. Keep the skits short—three to five minutes is usually enough.
* If possible, include a real customer in your enactment, to add depth and authenticity. Show the customer problem and the positive experience your solution delivers.
* Use video: Make a video recording of the skit. You can edit it and show it multiple times.

The Process of Innovation

No one is smart enough to think through all aspects of a solution. Rapid prototyping is part of a larger redefinition of innovation and the learning required to succeed. Early in the innovation process, we need to:

* Shift from selling the idea to learning from feedback.
* Redefine success to embrace failure and honor the learning it provides.
* Learn from doing, and do it quickly and cheaply.

As Tom Kelley, General Manager of IDEO has said, "Fail often to succeed sooner." (Kelley and Littman, 2001: p. 230)

Discovery

At its heart, prototyping is about discovery.

"The classical model of discovery is as follows: you search for what you know (say, a new way to reach India) and find something you didn't know was there (America)." Nassim Nicholas Taleb, *The Black Swan* (2007: p. 166)

CO-STAR Software: Online Innovation and Collaboration

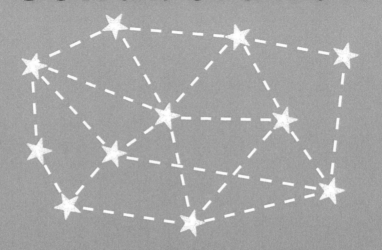

10.

CO-STAR Software: Online Innovation and Collaboration

In addition to the traditional face-to-face feedback conversations and RIIS sessions, we are now also able to collaborate online. Social media and crowdsourcing have introduced a new era of ideas creation. Pioneering organizations are employing Web 2.0 software to harness the genius of the group, to enable collaboration far beyond teams that meet in the same place or at the same time. For example, the web-based Q+ Innovation Platform incorporates CO-STAR into its application to enable you to share your ideas and CO-STARs online. You can gather feedback from any group, anywhere in the world.

If you are fortunate enough to operate in this type of enlightened innovation ecosystem, then you will have an opportunity to submit ideas online, as well as provide input and vote for the ideas of others.

Similar to many Idea management systems, Q+ participants can rate and rank ideas, so that the strongest ideas rise to the top. However, users can also add their CO-STAR value propositions and invite online feedback. Instructions and videos within the application teach CO-STAR basics, and guide users to enter SMART feedback, to specifically comment on the C, O, S, T, A, and R. Innovators can take the first round of feedback, integrate it into their thinking, and post a new version of their CO-STAR as soon as it is complete. Participants then get the chance to see how their feedback was helpful, as they see their own thinking integrated into a new, improved value proposition.

As an innovator, you can decide who to invite to comment on your CO-STAR. You can limit the feedback for your CO-STAR to subject-matter experts or use the "wisdom of the crowd."

Innovation Campaigns

Companies can use Q+ as well. They can run targeted innovation campaigns—issuing invitations to innovate within a specific area of strategic importance, with a two- to three-week window of time for collecting hundreds of ideas from employees. For example, project leaders could ask for CO-STARs for:

* Ongoing initiatives:
  * "How could we encourage suppliers to use Green materials?"
  * "How could we easily improve customer service?"

* Efforts to streamline, reduce waste, and cut costs:
  * "How could we reduce paperwork?"
  * "How could we make our recruiting process more efficient?"
  * "How could we streamline our approval process?"

* Strategic questions about opportunities for new products or services:
  * "How could we help busy families communicate?"
  * "What is a post office in the digital era? What products and services could it offer?"

Creating a Culture of Innovation

Organizations or groups using an online innovation platform like Q+ can create a lively, interactive culture of innovation. Tools like Q+ provide an intuitive and easy-to-use interface with single sign-on, searches, newsletters, blogs, polls, educational videos, or participant point systems to create an inspirational user experience. The goal is to make it fun and rewarding for individuals to join the community of innovators.

Points and Rewards

Many groups with online collaboration platforms offer points for adding ideas and CO-STARS, as well as points for voting or adding information to improve existing CO-STARs. People who contribute the most and the best ideas get visible recognition and rewards, along with those individuals who become well known for giving great advice. Each organization or social network may vary on the most coveted rewards, so prizes to innovators and advisors can be personalized. Financial rewards can be offered, but sometimes fame and visibility, access to key leaders, ability to choose projects, or joining advisory boards for helping to select other innovation projects can be just as motivating.

Polls, Surveys, Games

A poll or survey, or "Innovation Question of the Day" can keep people focused on the innovation challenges at hand. For example:

Question of the Day:
How did Thomas Edison light his laboratory?

Answer:
With electric lights. Edison did not invent the light bulb—the first electric light was actually invented in 1809 by Humphrey Davy, an English chemist, and the first light bulb was invented in 1854 by Henricg Globel, a German watchmaker. What Edison invented in 1879 was the system of innovation around the light bulb that made it easy to use. He improved each element of the

bulb itself, but he also had to create the electrical distribution system that carried power to the bulb, and even the light switches that enabled users to turn it on and off. (About.com, 2011)

Implications:
What system does your idea need around it to make it accessible and easy to use?

As one of our colleagues says, "A sparkle a day can keep people awake and focused. Let's keep people interested, intrigued, and 'in the game.'"

Photo or Video Campaigns

In the age of easy access to cameras on smartphones, participants can also be encouraged to add photos or videos to bring their ideas or comments to life. Or, for a particular innovation campaign or initiative, participants could show examples they encounter in their daily lives or examples they find from other industries. For example, in a campaign on improving customer service, a participant could submit a photo of a phone charger left behind in a hotel room after he checked out, when the hotel staff quickly notified him he had left it, and requested the best address to mail it to him. His lost charger arrived within two days and its photo went into the Q+ campaign.

Imagine a whole community of people on the lookout for examples of a particular kind of service or product or new opportunity. They may begin to notice great innovations wherever they occur. This becomes like an interactive game, a scavenger hunt where the everyday world provides plenty of examples of interesting innovations. Starting to see through the eyes of an innovator, while helping people engage in shared innovation initiatives and campaigns, can be fun.

CO-STAR SCORECARD

11.

CO-STAR SCORECARD

Once you have integrated the feedback you gathered, it is time to step back and make your own assessment. Like a movie critic, rate the quality of your idea to see if it is ready for release to the big screen. For each of the ten questions below circle the star on the scale of 1–10, where 1 = very little and 10 = a great deal.

1) To what degree have you clearly identified your customer?

1 ★ ★ ★ ★ ★ ★ ★ ★ ★ ★ 10

2) To what degree does your solution address a significant unmet customer need?

1 ★ ★ ★ ★ ★ ★ ★ ★ ★ ★ 10

3) To what degree does your solution represent a sizable opportunity worth pursuing?

1 ★ ★ ★ ★ ★ ★ ★ ★ ★ ★ 10

4) To what degree is your solution feasible?

1 ★ ★ ★ ★ ★ ★ ★ ★ ★ ★ 10

5) To what degree do you have the people in place to develop and deliver your solution?

1 ★ ★ ★ ★ ★ ★ ★ ★ ★ ★ 10

6) To what degree is your solution overwhelmingly superior to the competition?

1 ★ ★ ★ ★ ★ ★ ★ ★ ★ ★ 10

7) To what degree does your solution generate significant benefits for customers/users?

1 ★ ★ ★ ★ ★ ★ ★ ★ ★ ★ 10

8) To what degree does your solution generate substantial returns for sponsors/funders?

1 ★ ★ ★ ★ ★ ★ ★ ★ ★ ★ 10

9) To what degree is the timing right to pursue your solution?

1 ★ ★ ★ ★ ★ ★ ★ ★ ★ ★ 10

10) To what degree are you passionate about pursuing this solution?

1 ★ ★ ★ ★ ★ ★ ★ ★ ★ ★ 10

For every question, ask yourself: If not a 10, why not? _____
_____

What can you do to improve your rating? _____
_____

If you are an intrepreneur, you might also ask: Does your value proposition align with your company's business strategy? _____
_____

The scorecard offers a milestone decision point in your innovation effort. Review the progress you have made and the strengths and weaknesses of your CO-STAR. There is no shame in pulling the plug on this project and moving on to your next great idea.

On the other hand, if you are still passionate about your concept and believe it offers significant value, then it is time to create or refine your game plan. Based on the your overall score and insights from the individual ratings, where do you need to concentrate your energy? Create a game plan to complete your research, networking, quantification pitch, or prototype. What needs to be done, by whom, by when?

Once you have integrated the feedback from your network and community, you have built your CO-STAR to be as strong as it can be, and you are happy with the results from your own CO-STAR Scorecard assessment, this is a good time to stop and reflect:

- What has your CO-STAR taught you?
- What is the biggest surprise you found in turning your idea into a compelling value proposition?
- What would you advise a close friend or colleague who is just beginning the innovation process?
- Given all that you've learned, what would you most like to accomplish with your brilliant idea?
- What is the deepest value your idea can deliver?

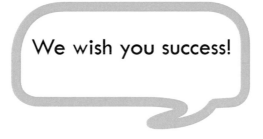

We wish you success!

Conclusion

12.
Conclusion

In companies and social networks that have introduced CO-STAR, this common discipline has quite naturally created a widely shared language of innovation. Innovators can quickly formulate their ideas around what customers need and the value their ideas will produce both for the organization and for its customers or users; they can pitch these value propositions to others; and they can get useful feedback from colleagues and customers to increase the value of their ideas. This continuous and often playful exchange of value propositions leads to a vibrant culture of innovation that inspires people to actively contribute to building the future.

Many diverse innovation tools, practices, and approaches are available in the marketplace. What is powerful is the agreement to use a similar tool because this enables rapid collaboration and value improvement among large numbers of people. Once innovators, partners, supporters, and funders speak the same innovation language, they can quickly get to work, focusing on their dreams.

CO-STAR, in combination with the Q+ online innovation platform, can help users to:

* Create targeted innovation campaigns to call for needed solutions.
* Gather information about important customer needs and market opportunities.
* Generate ideas and brainstorm solutions.
* Turn ideas into compelling value propositions.
* Pitch value propositions.
* Help recruit team members and resources needed.

* Gather focused and constructive feedback.
* Use collective intelligence to iterate and improve value propositions.
* Make a powerful sales pitch.
* Increase chances for selection, approval, and funding.
* Use wisdom of the crowd to help select the best value propositions.
* Serve as a guide for implementation.

At the personal level, recognize that championing your ideas is an inherently energizing activity; it engages your passion and stimulates your creativity. As you craft that initial CO-STAR and begin to build on its possibilities, you will most likely find yourself leaving your comfort zone to explore an exciting and fulfilling future that has yet to be defined. Being an innovator is being awake to new prospects for yourself, your organization, or even the larger world.

It is exciting to see a generation of innovators with unprecedented collaboration capabilities being born. Just think of the problems that will be solved and the value that will be created over the next few decades. This is the time for you and your idea to CO-STAR in a brighter future.

We are counting on you.

Appendix: CO-STAR Template

Use the template below to gather your thoughts and begin to prepare your pitch.

The Hook Start your pitch with a compelling question, fact, or statement that generates curiosity.	

C	Who are the **customers** and what are their needs?
O	What is the big **opportunity**?
S	What is your **solution**?
T	Who needs to be on the **team**?
A	What is your competitive **advantage**?
R	What **results** will you achieve?

The Request A specific request regarding next steps. A meeting? Resources?

ACKNOWLEDGMENTS

We want to give great thanks to Herman Gyr, our partner at EDG, who has been a co-creator of all of the ideas in this book. We also want to thank the innovators at Egmont UK who put these ideas to the test in their everyday work. They liked using CO-STAR so much in their own work that we decided to create the book together. Dawn Cordy and Kerrie Culff worked with us to develop this book from its initial concept all the way through to its final design. Leah James helped us with copy-editing and book layout, while Tiffany Leeson created the graphics and book design. One very innovative children's media team contributed the sample CO-STAR found in the middle of the book. They all made a wonderful team!

We want to thank Qmarkets, the software company that has helped us integrate CO-STAR into software that enables innovators to collaborate online. Our Q+ Innovation software guides innovators to post their CO-STARs online, to gather structured feedback and to give feedback to others, and to use collective intelligence to make their ideas stronger and stronger. With Q+, communities of people can collaborate to build and improve their CO-STARs across far-reaching geographies and time zones.

We also very much appreciate the contribution of sample CO-STARs from our colleagues. Thanks go to Roger Kirby, an innovator at Swisscom in Switzerland, for the Sustainable Shopper CO-STAR. The Families in Touch CO-STAR was contributed by the three co-founders of the organization—Steve Goddard, Ritch Partridge, and Mark McEvoy—along with Annamaria Willis from Cida Co, who first introduced these founders to CO-STAR. Cida Co often collaborates with EDG in teaching innovation strategy and skills. Cida Co works with governments, NGOs, and regional and local authorities to design and deliver strategies to grow their creative and knowledge economies, while also working with individuals to develop their entrepreneurial skills.

Many thanks also go to our EDG associates, clients, and colleagues, who have been important thinking partners—to Jasper Bousma from Vujade; Pierre Yves Cabboussat, VP of Innovation at Swiss Post; Tom Faure from Vibrant Enterprise Consulting; Matthias Müeller from Mensch Design Innovation in Switzerland; Ursula Osterle, VP of Innovation at Swisscom; Thomas Prehn from Asunto in Copenhagen, Denmark; and Christina Taylor, Head of Brand Experience at Swisscom. Thanks also go to our colleagues at CG-Innovation Partners in the US and the UK, who help put these concepts into action in building innovation ecosystems affiliated with their venture investments—to Jim Arnold, Stephen Lake, Michael Summers, and Jonathan Tudor—as well as to our very talented consulting and training associates in this CG-IP network, Carlos de Pommes and David Punchard. In addition, we appreciate the support and input from Brett Trusko, Assistant Professor of Medicine at Mount Sinai School of Medicine, and Associate Professor and one of the founding members of the Texas Institute for Smart Health at Baylor College of Medicine in Houston, Texas. Finally, we want to thank our wonderful and long-term affiliates from Ancilla Enterprise Development Consulting in the Philippines, Tita Puangco and her team, who provide innovative organization and business development solutions throughout Southeast Asia.

We are grateful to Curt Carlson, author of the book *Innovation* and CEO of SRI International (one of the largest independent R&D companies in the US and an innovation leader in Silicon Valley), and to Len Pollisotto, formerly of SRI and now vice-president of Strategic Business Development and Marketing at Draper Laboratories. We worked closely with both when we were faculty in SRI's innovation programs. We fondly recall Curt inspiring leaders who came to SRI from around the world, as he spoke to them about the essential role of innovators in solving the world's most important problems. We also learned from Len's constant commitment to require innovators to deliver quantitative value propositions. He could spot a fuzzy concept from a mile away and always pushed for specifics.

There are numerous models of value propositions available on books and websites, and we have tried to build on the thinking of many of these. We are grateful to Peter Drucker's classic HBR article, *The Discipline of Innovation*; Palo Alto's Institute for the Future's research on emerging trends a full decade ahead; IDEO's focus on customer experience design; Guy Kawasaki's many books, articles and videos about value propositions and pitching; Dealmaker Media's Under the Radar Pitching Competitions; and the many innovation speakers at Stanford's Technology Ventures Program, PARC, Sustainovation, and the MIT/Stanford Venture Lab.

Thanks also go to our hard-working, creative, and innovative clients at the BBC, Danish Broadcasting, Cida Co, Discovery Communications, EDF Energy, Philips Medical Systems, Stanford University, Swisscom, Swiss Post, Swiss TV, Texas Health Resources, The Work Foundation, and many others. Many of our clients are facing revolutions in their industries and are working to innovate a future none have ever seen before.

Most of all, we appreciate our families, for giving us the energy to write this book. Much love goes to Jannie and Herman, as well as to Alex and Cameron, and to Alex and Andreas, the next generation of young innovators.

BIBLIOGRAPHY

About.com (2011). *The Inventions of Thomas Edison*, available at: http://inventors.about.com/library/inventors/bledison.htm (accessed 11 August 2011).

BrainyQuote.com (no date), *Michelangelo Quotes*, available at: http://www.brainyquote.com/quotes/quotes/m/michelange161309.html (accessed 14 August 2011).

Carlson, C. and Wilmot, W. (2006). *Innovation: The Five Disciplines for Creating What Customers Want*. New York: Random House.

Chesbrough, H. (2003). *Open Innovation*. Boston, MA: Harvard Business School Press.

Drucker, P. (Nov–Dec 1998). *The Discipline of Innovation*. Boston, MA: Harvard Business Review.

Friedman, L. and Gyr, H. (1998). *The Dynamic Enterprise: Tools for Turning Chaos into Strategy and Strategy into Action*. San Francisco, CA: Jossey-Bass Business and Management Series/Wiley.

Johansson, F. (2006). *The Medici Effect: What Elephants and Epidemics Can Teach Us About Innovation*. Boston, MA: Harvard Business School Publishing.

IDEO (2011). *IDEO Method Cards for Customer Observation* [free iTunes app], available at: http://itunes.apple.com/gb/app/ideo-method-cards/id340233007?mt=8 (accessed 14 August 2011).

Kawasaki, G. (2004). *The Art of the Start*. New York: Penguin.

140

Kelley, T. and Littman, J. (2001). *The Art of Innovation: Lessons in Creativity from IDEO, America's Leading Design Firm*. New York: Currency Book/Random House.

Pinchot, G. (2001). *Intrapreneuring in Action*. San Francisco, CA: Berrett-Koehler.

Prahalad, C.K. and Ramaswamy, V. (2004). *The Future of Competition: Co-Creating Unique Value with Customers*. Boston, MA: Harvard Business School Press.

Taleb, N.N. (2007). *The Black Swan: The Impact of the Highly Improbable*. New York: Random House.

Wikipedia.org (2011). Tony Hseih, available at: http://en.wikipedia.org/wiki/Tony_Hsieh (accessed 14 August 2011).

Useful Value Proposition References:

Balland, J.-C. (2008). *Developing a Compelling Value Proposition*, available at: http://www.auxiliumtraining.com/ValueProposition2.htm (accessed 14 August 2011).

FutureLab.net (2011). *Marketing & Strategy Innovation*, available at: http://www.futurelab.net/blogs/marketing-strategy-innovation/2006/12/value_proposition_design_templ.html (accessed 14 August 2011).

Goldsbrough, M. (2003). *How to Craft Your Value Proposition*, available at: http://www.goldsbrough.biz/valueproposition (accessed 14 August 2011).

Shipley Associates (2006). *Value Propositions*, available at: http://www.shipleywins.com/library/26.pdf (accessed 14 August 2011).

Wikipedia.org (2011). *Value Proposition*, available at: http://en.wikipedia.org/wiki/Value_proposition (acessed 14 August 2011).

Index

Made in the USA
San Bernardino, CA
23 April 2019